The Best of
Harley-Davidson

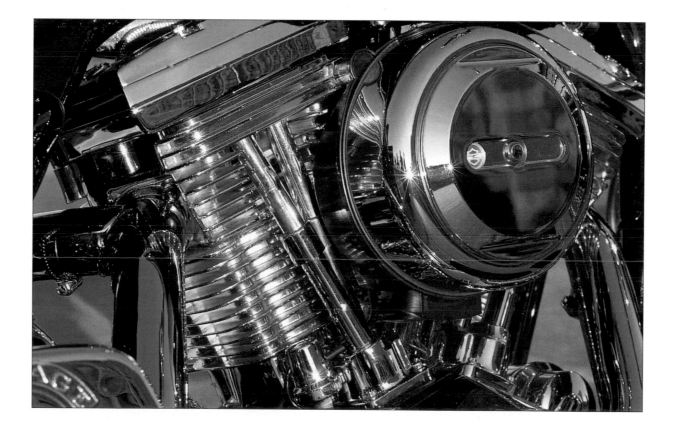

The Best of Harley-Davidson

Peter Henshaw

Photographs by Andrew Morland

Grange
BOOKS

Acknowledgments

As with any book, this one wouldn't have happened without the help of a great many people. First of all, my thanks go to all those Harley owners who allowed Andrew to photograph their bikes: Marilyn Meloche, Mark Bently, Steve Bass, Mallard Teal and all the others. Thanks also to Iain Cottrell of Military Harley-Davidson, the Harley-Davidson 45 Club (for information: contact Dean Roblett, 70B Parkview Road, New Eltham, London SE9 3EQ, United Kingdom) and to G.G. Buffing & Plating Inc. of Quebec, to Millers Custom Parts, the New Highlander Café (Florida), Pen Cycle Shop, Donnie Smith of Custom Cycle Fabrication and to Mike Terry of Old & Antique Motorcycles of Union, New Jersey. Most of the pictures were taken at Daytona Beach in 1996, the rest in various parts of the U.K. Thanks also to everyone at Regency House Publishing for taking the book on, to Lynne and Martin for lending me their Mac and to Neil, who put my Triumph back together while I was too busy writing.

Peter Henshaw, Andrew Morland
Somerset, England, March 1996

The Best of Harley-Davidson represents the private view of the author and is not an official Harley-Davidson publication.

Published in 1996 by
Grange Books
An imprint of Grange Books PLC
The Grange, Grange Yard
London SE1 3AG

Designed by Annabel Trodd

Printed in China

CONTENTS

Page 1
G.G. Buffing did the gold plating as well as all the chrome work and polishing on this machine. Many of the custom houses use actual completed bikes to advertise their work – it's a lot more effective than any number of leaflets.

Pages 2-3
Massive studded leather saddlebags and seat are standard Harley accessories, bought from any dealer. Actually none of this is new – dealers were selling genuine Harley-Davidson saddlebags in the 1920s.

These pages
The Road King's detachable screen held in by spring clips (so no spanners needed) was so successful that Harley launched a whole range of detachable accessories – luggage racks, sissy bars and screens which could be installed or removed in less than a minute.

No one is neutral about Harley-Davidson – most motorcyclists either love them or ... they don't. Certainly no one (whether they ride or not) can claim not to know the name. Why is the image so strong, the recognition so instantaneous? After all, Harleys have rarely been at the cutting edge of two-wheel technology.

Age has a lot to do with it – Harley-Davidson has been around longer than any other motorcycle manufacturer. Others may have started earlier, but most have since fallen by the wayside, or kept going in fits and starts – Harley-Davidson has been making motorcycles without a break since 1903. It's this continuity that helps to explain the strong image.

But there's something else as well: through wars, depressions and technical change, Harley-Davidson has stuck with the V-twin. If it never built the most powerful or innovative V-twin, it can at least claim to have a special relationship with what is in many ways the ideal engine for a motorcycle. There have been other makers whose names have been synonymous with V twins – Ducati, Vincent-HRD, and Moto-Guzzi – but none have been around for quite as long, or made as many bikes. If it's possible to have degrees of synonymity, then the name of Harley-Davidson is more synonymous with V-twins than anyone else's.

The V-twin has virtually become a Harley-Davidson trademark. The company has dabbled with other engines – singles have come and gone since the very beginning, but they haven't offered one for seventeen years. There have been flat twins too, as well as plans for straight fours and sixes. But in the end, Harley-Davidson has always come back to what it knows best.

Not that it has ever been a V-twin innovator. Harley's technical history is punctuated, less by inspirational leaps than by steady, go-with-the-flow progress. Bill Harley's first V-twin came at a time when most American manufacturers were doing exactly the same. The move to side-valves followed Indian's lead, and while Harley introduced an overhead-valve V-twin before Indian, ohv was commonplace at the time. Cycle parts too, only progressed as the market did – telescopic forks, swing-arm suspension, 12-volt electrics and electric start, all came in gradually.

Harley has always been a conservative company. Right from the start, Bill Harley and the three Davidson brothers were concerned with making a solid, reliable motorcycle, nothing too fancy. That innate conservatism has been a feature of the company ever since. There have been some highlights, like the fast, good-looking Knucklehead of the 1930s, and the early Sportsters, but they are the exceptions.

Still, it's done them no harm. Harley-Davidson today is successful precisely because of its decades of steady progress. That continuity has given it an appealing solidity as a company with roots and a lineage. For the thousands of bikers looking to buy something with some heritage behind it, the appeal is strong. Now you might say that this is just a clever way of foisting outdated bikes onto a gullible public, but there are plenty out there who think differently.

Left: *This bike, one of the last Shovelheads, is a product of Cole Custom Cycles. In their own words: 'It started life as a 1982 Harley-Davidson FLH Classic, and the bike was purchased as a basket case. Starting from the front, the wheel and rotor are by RC Engineering, and the brakes are by Jaybrake...'*

Far left:'*... the motor is now 84 inches [2.13m], totally rebuilt by Mike Brown, the cam is S& S, along with the carb, and the pipes are Bartels. There is a pair of Dyna coils for ignition, on a Cycle Fab bracket ...'*

Far left: '*... the fenders are Sumax Street Sweepers, the tank was stretched by a friend (named Tank) who also made the console and the seat base...'*

Left: '*... the tranny is also new with a total polish job and the engine cases are polished as well. The swing arm is a Ness piece, and the rear brakes are Jaybrake with a homemade bracket ...'*

Chapter One
Right First Time: F & J Twins

The Harley-Davidson Motor Company did not invent the V-twin. Neither was its first twin the fastest, smoothest or the most advanced. On the other hand, it was less likely to fall apart than most of the opposition which made it, if not unique, then at least rather special.

Still, when Bill Harley drew up the first Harley-Davidson Vee, he can have had no idea he was about to found a dynasty. In his methodical, logical way, he was simply pursuing the sensible course that most major rivals were following. Half a dozen years after the first practicable motorcycles clattered and shook their way onto the roads, riders began to want more power. This was especially true in America where towns were further apart and the roads rougher and more demanding.

The obvious solution was to increase engine size, but the current 35ci (575cc) singles had reached the practical limits possible from just one cylinder. So another cylinder was needed and the easiest way to do that was simply to cut a second hole in the top of the crankcase and bolt on another single. Strengthen the cases to suit, connect both conrods to a common crankshaft, juggle with the valve and ignition arrangements to serve two cylinders rather than one and, hey presto! a V-twin of double the single's capacity and presumably double its power as well.

It was a particularly neat solution in that most of the single's components could still be re-used, while the V-twin would often sit conveniently inside an existing frame. Indian, Thor and countless others took the same route and the Harley-Davidson Founders knew that they'd have to as well.

So when Bill Harley completed his

engineering degree and came back to Milwaukee to take up where he left off, a V-twin was one of the first things on his mind. It was typical of the thorough approach of Harley and the Davidsons that one of them would take three years off to get some proper training. Despite his degree, Bill's first V-twin wasn't an unqualified success. It first appeared at a cycle show in late 1907, but didn't go on sale for nearly another two years. Even then, it rather proved to be little more powerful than the single. How different it was to that first bike, which Harley and the Davidsons had taken so long to perfect. Harley's first twin was basically a combination of two of the inlet-over-exhaust singles, but with a slightly smaller bore to give 49ci (800cc). It used Harley-Davidson's own carburettor or a Schebler, and the Founders claimed 7hp and a top speed of 65mph (105km/h) – heady stuff!

Unfortunately, it didn't quite work out like that. One legacy of the single's cylinder was an automatic inlet valve which opened by suction as the piston moved down and which wasn't positively pushed open by a pushrod and rocker. This was actually standard practice at the time, at least for low-powered bikes, and one school of thought held it to be superior   opening only when there was a vacuum in the cylinder, it should have variable timing, whereas a pushrod-operated valve had fixed timing.

But whatever theoretical advantages the automatic valve may have had, they were negated by the fact that it limited the engine to about 500rpm. As single and twin Harleys had similar gearing, this meant that the new bike wouldn't go any faster than the old one, which was hardly the idea. Then there was another legacy from the single – belt drive. Even the twin's meagre reserves of power were enough to make the belt slip, and there was no means of

Opposite: *Everyone knows Harley for its V-twins, but the men from Milwaukee started off making singles. This 1921 21ci (344cc) single was made when twins dominated Harley-Davidson, as they would for the rest of the century.*

Left: *The dark green paintwork was by Gilles Sauvageau and Yvan Jodoin. The vast array of paints and lacquers available today makes more variety easier to achieve – a far cry from the Silent Gray Fellows.*

tightening it. This, together with the lack of performance, was enough to kill the first twin, few of which were sold. The single, on the other hand, went on selling like proverbial hot cakes – 154 were sold in 1907, 450 the year after, then over 1,000, then more than 3,000. But Harley Davidson still needed a twin.

The Company came back for another go in 1911, but this time it seemed to have got it right. Still belt drive (but with a tensioning system), still using the same ioe arrangement (but with proper mechanical inlet valves). Power was a (more realistic) claimed 6.5 hp. And like the singles, the '6-D' (Harley-Davidson wasn't given to evocative model names in those early days) was solid, well-built and reliable. It used a quality Bosch magneto, and when they arrived, Harley-Davidson's own electrics were to establish a good name for reliability as well. As with the single, the Harley-Davidson twin wasn't the fastest bike you could buy, nor the cheapest nor the flashiest, but it did keep going. And it soon gained a classic Harley-Davidson capacity in 1912 when it was bored out to 61ci (1000cc).

The forks were Harley-Davidson's own leading links which Harley had designed while away at college and which had been fitted to the singles from 1907. The solid, unsprung legs were mounted just behind the sprung ones, with four long coil springs enclosed within the movable fork. It was the famous Springer whose basic design was to stay with Harley-Davidson until 1949. Unlike the cartridge forks favoured by Indian and others, the leading links didn't vary the bike's wheelbase as they worked, though travel was only just over an inch in those first ones. The rear end was rigid of course; it would be years before Harley-Davidson got round to fitting rear suspension.

Lubrication was the usual total-loss system: after the oil had done its job, the engine just burnt it, which saved on oil changes but made for a smoky exhaust. It fell by gravity from the combined fuel/oil tank through a glass sight-tube to the crankcase, where it took care of the crank and bearings. The moving parts would force it up to the piston and lower cylinder wall; and anything not burned in the combustion chamber fell back to the bottom of the crankcase for periodic draining. This gravity system was supplemented by a hand operated oil pump from 1912. Automatic oil pumps were still years away, and the chief problem with the hand pump was that of over-concerned owners over-lubing the engine!

But the real advances were about to come in transmission design. In the years leading up to the First World War, motorcycle design was still in its infancy, with new ideas coming thick and fast. As with any fast-developing technology, each improvement increased the pressure for more change – an advance in one area soon revealed limitations in another. Now that engines were developing more power, the drawbacks of the basic belt-drive became more obvious, notably the crude tensioning system and its inability to drive the bike up hills.

This was especially true of American bikes, which had got bigger and faster than those in Europe; the result was a brief, golden age of innovation. For Harley, the big change came in 1912, with chain drive for the twins. Other bikes had already gone over to chains, but Bill Harley refused to countenance the move until he had a suitable clutch to go with it.

He came up with a substantial multi-plate device with 76 sq inches of plate surface. Mounted in the rear hub, it was controlled by a hand lever on the left (some say the right) of the fuel tank, and allowed riders to make hitherto unheard of smooth stops and starts. Other manufacturers were using a proprietary clutch called the Eclipse which was mounted on the engine pulley, though it wasn't as long-lived as the Harley-Davidson version.

Best of all, the Milwaukee multi-plate (as they might well have called it) allowed Harley V-twins to use that far more efficient chain drive. There was a primary chain as well, oiled by mist from the crankcase vent. It all made starting easier, as instead of having to pedal the bike up to speed until the engine fired, the machine could now be fired up on its stand. You just gave the engine a little time to warm up, disengaged the clutch, rolled the bike off its stand, and you were away. This was followed up in 1914 with a two-speed gearbox inside the rear hub. Three sets of bevel gears did the trick, as long as they were greased every 1,500 miles (2414km) or so. The important point was that with a choice of ratios, the engine could be tuned for more revs and power – another technical bottleneck overcome!

The following year there were yet more improvements. The two-speed hub was replaced by a three-speed box using sliding gears. Mounted behind the clutch where the primary and final chains met, it was another step closer to the modern motorcycle transmission. This basic layout of two chains and a gearbox was here to stay until Harley returned to belt drive (albeit of a more sophisticated sort) with the Sturgis, sixty-five years later.

The year 1915 saw the introduction of an automatic oil pump and the new Remy magneto-

Opposite: Gold-plated wheels and engine? Whatever would Bill Harley and the Davidsons, the Founding Fathers, have thought of that?

generator system (the rear light was detachable for use as an inspection light), and the old bicycle-style pedals were replaced by a proper kick starter. Meanwhile, engine development hadn't stood still – bigger inlet ports, manifold and carburettor meant more power. Harley-Davidson now claimed 16.7hp from dynamometer tests, and guaranteed 11hp for every twin.

In 1916, as the Model J, this became the definitive ioe twin which was to stay in production until 1929, by which time it was well past its sell-by date. It had certainly come a long way since the first abortive 1909 Vee, and had taken Harley-Davidson through a tumultuous period in American motorcycle history, when technical progress was rapid and competition fierce. But having come through all that, and helped establish Harley-Davidson as one of the Big Three manufacturers, the J seemed to reach a plateau. There were no major innovations for the rest of its life, which was to teach Harley a hard lesson in keeping up with the competition.

Specifications

1915 Model 11J

Engine	*Inlet-over-exhaust, 45-degree V-twin*
Bore x stroke	*3 $^5/_{16}$ x 3 $^1/_2$in (84.1 x 88.9mm)*
Capacity	*60.33ci (988cc)*
Connecting rods	*Male/female type, with roller-bearing big end and bushed small end*
Lubrication	*Total loss, pumped by integral drivecase cover and oiler with supplementary hand pump*
Power	*11hp*
Gearbox	*Three-speed, sliding gears*
Primary drive	*Chain*
Clutch	*Dry, multiplate*
Final drive	*Chain*
Suspension	
Front	*Leading-link forks*
Rear	*Rigid*
Brakes	
Front	*None*
Rear	*Coaster type, operated by right-hand pedal*
Wheels/tyres	*3.00 x 22in*
Wheelbase	*59 $^1/_2$in (151cm)*
Weight	*325lb (147kg)*
Fuel capacity	*1 $^7/_8$ gallons (9 litres)*
Fuel consumption	*50mpg (141 ltr/km) est.*
Top speed	*60mph (97km/h) est.*

The first V-twin (the 11F) had a prolonged and painful birth, but developed into a very reliable bike. The ioe engine was not state-of-the-art, but chain final drive and proper gearbox were.

Chapter Two

Follow That: The VL

Follow ups are never easy, especially when, as in the case of the Harley V-series, they come after a well-loved predecessor. But the VL's introduction wasn't so much difficult as a disaster. Of course, even if the new side valve twin had been impeccable from the start, there would no doubt have been diehard fans of the old J who wanted nothing to do with it: this sort of engineering snobbery is common to all generations. As it was, the new bike didn't even have the traditional Harley-Davidson virtues to recommend it, at least at first. Compared to the old model it was slow and unwieldy, and it had fundamental engine problems.

But all that was in the future when the four Founders laid out the design for the new bike. The J-series had been around for years and its inlet-over-exhaust valve arrangement hailed back to the very first Harleys. Now, Indians and Excelsiors were leaving the big Milwaukee twin for dead, both on the road and on the track. Harley-Davidson needed a new engine to compete, but the big question was, should it go for side-valves, or overheads?

Overhead valve was the coming technology: it allowed engines to rev higher and harder, and the leading edge British bikes were using it. But Harley-Davidson took what seems like a retrograde step: it went for side-valves.

There were actually good reasons for doing so. At the time, overhead valves were still exposed to the open air, so they were noisy, messy, oily things that lubricated one's trousers and didn't suit Harley-Davidson's sensible touring image. They wore out quickly, and if a valve dropped (not unknown), mechanical chaos ensued. Side-valves on the other hand, were

Opposite: The side-valve VL was intended to keep up with the Indians that were humiliating Harley on road and track. Unfortunately, early VLs were an embarrassment in themselves.

Right: Great things were claimed for the V-series side-valve V-twin. But far from the promised 15-20 per cent power increase, it produced only 1hp more than the old J-series.

quieter and enclosed. The engines were cheaper to make and, with detachable cylinder heads, easier to repair than the inlet-over-exhaust set-up, while the decoking ritual became a Sunday morning pleasure. But perhaps most significant for Harley, the Indian Scout 61 and 74ci (1000 and 1200cc) Chiefs, which were all proving decisively quicker than any Harley, all used side-valves.

That was all quite understandable, but when the new V-series was announced in August 1929, there were other doubts that the bike might not be, as Harley-Davidson trumpeted, 'The greatest achievement in motorcycle history'. It still used the J's total-loss lubrication system which really was obsolete by this time (not until 1936 would Harley-Davidson go over to a proper recirculating system). With its new engine, frame and forks, it was also much heavier than the old J it replaced: 529lb (240kg) against 408lb (185kg).

Even that wouldn't have mattered so much had Harley's claims of 15-20 per cent more power been accurate – they weren't. According to the factory's own power curves, the VL produced 30hp at 4,000rpm, just 1hp more than the equivalent JDH. The lower compression (4:1) V made 28hp against the JDL's 26 hp.

On paper, at least, they should have been slightly faster, but in give and take driving on the road, they were anything but. It wasn't just the greater poundage that made the Vs less sprightly than the JDH: to improve their already sluggish acceleration, the V bikes had been given very small flywheels, which actually blunted performance over about 50mph (80km/h) and caused eyeball-shaking vibration at any speed.

The Buffalo police were so disgusted with their new Vs that William H. Davidson had to rush down there and do a quick overhaul only days after delivery. He replaced valves, springs, pistons and silencers, among other things. According to William, he then proved all was well by taking one officer for a 75-mph (121-km/h) spin in a sidecar outfit – the officer was convinced.

But it wasn't just the police who weren't happy. Milwaukee was inundated with letters, calls and telegrams castigating the new bike and pleading for the old one (especially the almost legendary Two Cam) to be brought back. 'Uneconomic', said the factory, which instead started a crash redesign programme for the V, during which the bike was actually taken off sale for four months. It emerged with hefty new flywheels, which needed bigger crankcases to accommodate them, which in turn needed a different frame.

In other words, every V-series had to be almost completely dismantled and rebuilt. Kits of parts were sent out to dealers which Harley paid for, on condition that the dealers fitted them at their own expense. For some, this was the last straw: Harley-Davidson's attitude to dealers was traditionally regarded as autocratic, and some resented being lumbered with the quality control role in addition to their usual selling activities. But it was an expensive business for the company as well as for the dealers: over 1,300 bikes had to be rebuilt: the new parts alone cost over $100,000. Only royalty fees from Alfred Rich Child (who was building Harleys under licence, in Japan) saved Harley-Davidson from digging deeper into its reserves.

Fortunately, as with every other Harley whose early life was troubled, the V bikes evolved into thoroughly reliable mounts. No one could pretend that the V was a sportster, but after a few years, many riders began to accept that here was another solid touring twin just as the J had been. It may have been heavy, but the VL was capable of a genuine 85mph (137km/h). The diminishing coterie of Two Cam diehards might maintain that their bikes could each touch 100mph (160km/h), but that was a best-case boast. A thoroughly fettled Two Cam, well ridden, might touch the ton, but not all of them were. The V by contrast, could keep up 70-75mph (113-121km/h) reliably. Veteran Harley dealer Tom Sifton later recalled how on club runs the side-valve VLs and 45s would keep going while the much-vaunted Js either overheated or shook themselves apart.

The V had other advantages. The new duplex primary chain was stronger than the old one and it had automatic metred lubrication; both wheels were at once quickly detachable and interchangeable (though on early bikes the rear wheel splines caused trouble); the seat height was comfortably low; and the electrics maintained Harley-Davidson's good reputation in this area, with a 22-amp battery, sealed coil and high frequency horn. You could have the bike with either generator or magneto (in which case it was a VM or VLM respectively) and there was a package truck option as well as the usual sidecar version. In Japan, they built up a sort of forerunner to the Servicar, by ordering VLs from Milwaukee with extra long rear chains and no rear wheels. Despite all its problems, Harley-Davidson managed to sell over 10,000 V bikes in 1930, so the public can't have been completely put off.

The trouble was, just as the V seemed to be finding its feet, the Depression began to take

the Two Cam JDH was introduced in 1933. Its secret was magnesium alloy pistons which, together with new cylinders and heads, gave a compression ratio of 5:1. Perhaps even more significant was that buyers now had a choice of colours. It might not seem such a big deal now, but for years William Harley and the Davidsons followed the Henry Ford school of colour choice. All the early bikes were grey, and after the First World War, olive green was the like-it or lump-it shade (with some sober pinstriping, if you were lucky).

But in 1933, the few people who bought new Harleys could choose between silver and turquoise with black and gold striping, black and mandarin red with gold striping, sunshine blue and white (more gold striping), or police blue and white, again with gold highlights. Olive

Far left: In the 1930s, most American bikes were still in the hand-gearchange era. Note the ammeter, with its neat, free-standing light, though Harley-Davidson electrics were more reliable than most.

Left: There were some genuine improvements over the J, though. The duplex primary chain had a metred oil supply and the engine was easier to maintain than before.

Below: A simple but effective Harley-Davidson badge on the tank. Countless different graphics were to grace Harley-Davidson tanks over the years, but the basic arrangement of the name remained the same.

hold. Although the bike was launched only a couple of months before the Wall Street Crash, at first it looked as if the American economy would be largely unaffected by these stock market shenanigans, and certainly Harley managed to sell over 17,000 bikes in 1930. But three years on, with a third of the working population without work, and usable Model Ts on offer for a pittance, less than 7,000 bikes were sold and 3,700 the year after. The motorcycle had become a luxury item, which was all very well when times were good, but in the middle of a depression most people were more concerned with keeping the roof over their heads, and filling

their stomachs.

Still, Harley-Davidson survived, but only just. At one Board meeting the four Founders seriously discussed giving up altogether: the Milwaukee complex they had worked so hard to build up was working at just 10 per cent of its capacity. In the end, they decided to economize rather than close down: the industrial engine business was abandoned, men were laid off and salaries were cut while the racing effort was curtailed altogether.

Meanwhile, there was a concerted effort to freshen up the V-series. The VLD, a 36hp machine that finally matched the performance of

Right: *Although most V-series bikes used a 74ci (1,207cc) version of the side-valve twin, an 80ci (1311cc) 39-hp alternative came along in 1935. A four-speed gearbox was introduced that year as well.*

Opposite: *Engine, frame and forks were all new for the V-series, but around 1,300 of them had to be completely rebuilt to fulfil their original promise costing Harley-Davidson $100,000 in parts alone.*

green still lurked in the background, but only if complemented by brilliant green and matching pinstripes. The whole colourful ensemble was set off by a beautiful art deco bird motif, perhaps the most stylish design ever to grace a Harley-Davidson tank!

The introduction of colours was actually a reaction to circumstance. Arch-rival Indian had almost collapsed which would have left Harley-Davidson as the dominant motorcycle maker in the States. But at the last minute, it was saved by industrialist E. Paul Du Pont who did more than provide Indian with a firm financial backing. Paint was part of the Du Pont empire, so Indians now came in a range of bright colours. Rivalry between the two firms was so intense (they'd been battling for leadership of the U.S. market for nearly twenty years) that Harley had no choice but to follow suit.

So intense was the competition that it led to some of the less salubrious chapters in Harley history. Harley-Davidson dealers were allegedly given $20 in cash if they junked a part-exchanged Indian or Excelsior. Then there was the police sales scandal. According to Harry Sucher (author of *The Milwaukee Marvel*) it was Walter Davidson's idea to offer the VL to the police at virtually cost price, any trade-in machines being junked. Milwaukee seemed desperate to run the competition off the road. However, there was still some mutual back-scratching going on, and every year top people from Harley and Indian would meet to fix prices. It was at one of these meetings that E. Paul du Pont turned up unexpectedly. After a clearing of the air, he reportedly shook hands with Walter Davidson, who apologized for some of the more personal insults to have come out of Harley-Davidson.

Right: A slim, simple profile belies the mass of the V-series. The VL actually weighed over 100lb (45kg) more than the J-series it replaced. Even by modern standards it was a heavy machine

Opposite: This 1934 V (also owned by Steve Slocombe) came with its original styling, but a few years later all the side-valves were to be redesigned along Knucklehead lines.

Meanwhile, the V bikes were gradually updated – 1935 saw an optional four-speed transmission and a new 80ci (1300cc) version. The Eighty was really no more than the existing Seventy-Four, bored out for extra capacity and 39hp in high compression form. The Eighty was a response to police demands for more power, and with sidecar use in mind. It was no sportster: that role was reserved for the imminent ohv Knucklehead – instead, it continued the Harley tradition of solid, reliable tourers. It also underlined Harley-Davidson's fondness for certain engine sizes – 54, 61, 74 and 80ci (883, 1000, 1200 and 1300cc) versions are all well established.

The flash new Knucklehead soon overshadowed these side-valve bikes, but they fought back in 1937 with Knucklehead styling and dry-sump lubrication. The latter in particular was a big step forward from the prehistoric total loss system – riders had to get used to changing the oil every now and again, but at least it was circulating properly. The bikes got a new name, the U-series (Harley-Davidson never gave its bikes names in those pre-war years, hence the profusion of nicknames). The basic U was the low compression 74 and the UL was the same bike with 5.5:1 compression, while the equivalent 80s were designated UH and ULH respectively.

These changes marked a final era of respectability for the big sidevalvers – it was somehow symbolic that William Connelly and Fred Dauria had attempted a transcontinental record on VLs. They were sidelined by breakdowns, but they succeeded the following year when their U model and sidecar held together for the 3,000 mile crossing. The outfit wasn't promising – weighed down by a mountain of spare parts, its top speed was just 58mph (93km/h). Fred and William started late in the year, so they had to cope with freezing weather over the Rocky Mountain passes. They would ride for 300 miles (483km) each and stop for fuel every 600 miles (966km). After a total of 69 hours and 46 minutes, they rode triumphantly into Los Angeles, setting a record which was to stand for twenty years. Harley-Davidson's troublesome side-valve had come good at last.

Specifications

1930 V/VL

Engine	Side-valve 45-degree V-twin
Bore x stroke	3 $\frac{7}{16}$ x 4in (87.3 x 101.6 mm)
Capacity	73.66ci (1207cc)
Compression ratio	V 4.5:1/VL 5.0:1
Power	V 28hp @ 4,000rpm VL 30hp @ 4,000rpm
Gearbox	Three-speed, sliding gear
Clutch	Dry, multi-plate (metal lined discs)
Primary drive	Duplex chain, oil-mist lubricated
Final drive	Chain
Suspension	
Front	Leading-link springer forks
Rear	Rigid
Brakes	
Front	None
Rear	Coaster type, operated by right-hand pedal
Wheels/tyres	
Front	4.00 x 19in, quickly detachable
Rear	4.40 x 19in, quickly detachable
Wheelbase	60 in (152cm)
Seat height	28 in (71cm)
Weight	529lb (240kg)
Fuel capacity	4 gallons (18 litres)
Fuel consumption	35-50mpg (13-18 ltr/km)
Top speed (estimated)	V 80mph/VL 85mph (129/137km/h)

Chapter Three
Knucklehead: A Great Leap Forward

Every motorcycle manufacturer, famous for either a succession of legends or lemons, has a milestone bike, something which represents a real break from the past and the start of a new line. It might not be the fastest thing they ever made, nor the most beautiful, nor even the most technically advanced, but in the case of the Harley-Davidson Knucklehead, it was all three.

And that wasn't all. Not only was the Knucklehead (officially, it was known less evocatively as the '61E') faster than any other production Harley at the time, it was better looking and bang up-to-date. There were a few other reasons why it was a milestone in Harley history.

It represented a final victory over Indian. The feud between Springfield and Milwaukee had been going on for over twenty years. It seemed that neither would be satisfied until it had achieved complete market domination over the other. In some ways, Harley-Davidson had already caught and passed Indian before the Knucklehead came along. At the low point of the Depression, in 1933, Harley sold only 3,700 machines, but Indian a catastrophic 1,657. And it had long been accepted that while Indians were faster than Harleys, they didn't hold together as well. It was common practice for racing Indians to use Harley bottom ends to combine top end performance and long-term durability. Indian Scouts were far quicker than Milwaukee's 45, but many used pistons from Harley's 21ci (344cc) single, to make sure they stayed that way.

The Knucklehead was a change of image for Harley too. From the start, the four Founders were determined to make, not the fastest motorcycle, but the most dependable. That slow

but reliable image (side-valve troubles notwithstanding) had stuck. Harleys might not be fast or flash, but they always got you there in the end. It had become the tourists' choice, perhaps even an old man's bike. The Knucklehead changed all that – it was really the first sportster, years before the Sportster came along, and it gave the company a 95mph (153km/h) flagship. It even took Harley-Davidson back into official competition, via Joe Petrali's taking of the mile speed record at Daytona.

Finally, it was a statement of faith in the future as far as the four Founders were concerned. Arthur, Walter and William Davidson, and Bill Harley, were all approaching retirement age by the time the Knucklehead went on sale. Over thirty years of hard work had seen them rise from garden shed to market domination. Their innate caution, and their insistence on making bikes that were solid and reliable rather than innovatory, had paid off handsomely. Yet here they were in the middle of the worst depression for generations, about to make a massive investment in an all-new bike that could bankrupt the company. Why did they do it?

It's worth remembering that the Depression hit Harley-Davidson hard. The company sold over 20,000 bikes in 1929, the year of the Wall Street Crash, but half that number in 1931. For 1932, though 9,000 were planned, only 6,800 left the gates and production halved again the year after. There were the inevitable redundancies, with workers more likely to face the soup kitchen than an alternative job. The Founders cut their own salaries in half; we know from records of Board meetings that they had seriously considered a complete close-down, though having amassed their respective fortunes, the

Harley and Davidson families would doubtless have been financially secure, even if they had closed down and sold up.

But despite their age, and the financial risks involved, they went ahead with the development of the Knucklehead. For these practical, hard working, self-made men to simply give up would have been unthinkable. So it was with no small amount of foresight, not to mention courage, that they pressed on with what was, by Harley-Davidson standards, a radically new motorcycle.

The Board gave the go-ahead in August 1931, with the aim of having the new bike ready for the 1935 model year, so it would have to be on sale in late 1934. It wasn't, for several reasons, not least of which was that the design department had suffered as many cuts as the others: there just weren't enough staff to get such a major, all-new project moving fast enough. What engineers there were were prevented from working overtime by the National Recovery Administration, a government body which required men without work to be given jobs rather than letting the lucky ones work overtime. There was also a 31ci (500cc) ohv single under development at the same time. In the end it came to nothing, but at the time there was some indecision as to whether the company should go ahead with this or the V-twin, which complicated matters. And finally, there were the inevitable development problems.

According to Harry Sucher, much of the practical development work was actually done by Joe Petrali and Hank Syvertson of the Racing Department, assisted by Bill Harley's son, William J. Harley. William was expected to start at the bottom, so he worked as an apprentice while studying for an engineering degree. More

to the point, he helped out with development riding on the Knucklehead. William was to later recall a number of near accidents, until the prototype's fork geometry was changed. There were other problems too. The new overhead valve engine was in a frame by May 1934 and produced plenty of power. But it had terrible oil leaks from the top end, mainly because no attempt had been made to enclose the valve springs and stems.

Joe Petrali wanted the launch date postponed to sort this out, or at least to have a pilot run before full production started. But the bike was already a year overdue, and Walter Davidson was determined that they would adhere to the new launch date of June 1936. There was also the matter of dry sump lubrication, one of the bike's new features, which had been upstaged by Indian. Springfield had introduced its own dry sump in 1933 and Walter knew that to delay any further risked the same thing happening again with some other feature. Harley-Davidson dealers wanted the new bike, too. They were shown a prototype at the 1935 dealer convention, and they went wild. On the other hand, Walter Davidson and the Board no doubt had the VL and 45 fiascos still fresh in their minds, so they compromised. The Knucklehead was launched on time, but in a very low-key way. There was no great fanfare, and Harley-Davidson stressed to its dealers that this was a limited production bike not intended for mass consumption.

They needn't have worried. The Knucklehead was a roaring success, selling 1,900 in its first year. Technically, it didn't just bring Harley up to date with its competitors, it leapfrogged ahead of them. The key point was the overhead valves, which allowed the engine to rev higher and produce more power than any previous road-going V-twin from Milwaukee. Harley-Davidson had made ohv bikes before, but they were either handmade racers or conversions of existing side-valve or F-head engines. The Knucklehead was designed from the start for ohv.

Overhead valves had actually been around for years, but only now were they becoming practicable for road bikes. Fuel was increasing in quality and octane rating, so the ohv's greater efficiency and potential for higher compression ratios could be used to advantage. The Knucklehead's overheads were controlled by a single, four-lobe camshaft and double-valve springs. The dry sump system was a real step forward, too. Rather than suffer the uncertainties of the old total loss system (which had been around since the very beginning) the engine benefited from a properly metered and automatically provided supply of cool, fresh oil: the rider no longer had to give the engine an extra splurge of oil via the hand pump every now and then, but he did have to get used to the new chore of oil changes.

All this new technology meant that the Knucklehead compared well with state-of-the-art British V-twins like the JAP and the Matchless. Like them, it followed the trend towards shorter strokes, which allowed higher revs and hence more power. This development evidently worked, as the Knucklehead produced 40hp at 4,800rpm in high compression EL form. Such power and such engine speeds were light years away from the plodding VL side-valvers of old.

But the Knucklehead's impact wasn't just down to its engine, central to its success though

Right: It wasn't just that the Knucklehead was fast. It looked better than any previous Harley, though there's no evidence that it was ever 'styled' as such.

Opposite left: Changes to the frame geometry cured the wayward tendencies of some early prototypes, but engine oil leaks persisted at the production stage – Joe Petrali had wanted more pre-launch time to sort the bike out.

Oppsite right: The Knucklehead's nickname derived from the shape of its rocker covers, another Harley first. More to the point, it was powerful and revvy: just what Milwaukee needed to get ahead of Indian.

it was. Virtually every part of the bike was new, or produced in a new way. Even the fuel tank was welded together, rather than soldered. There were still leading link forks, but they were of new tubular section design rather than the old I-beams of the VL. The clutch design was new, and the four-speed gearbox was a constant-mesh version that was years ahead of the old sliding-gear type (which Indian was still using). The frame was new, too.

Finally, like any milestone bike, the Knucklehead simply looked right. In fact, it looked terrific. There's no evidence that Harley-Davidson deliberately styled this bike more than any of its others. From the start, the Founders were more concerned with how their bikes ran rather than how they looked, and had only recently taken the radical step of introducing a choice of colours. But whether it was deliberately introduced or not, the Knucklehead's styling worked, from its long, tapering tank to its swept-back rear mudguard. There was also the elegant, fuel tank-mounted speedometer of course, which was later to become a Harley-Davidson trademark. Perhaps its real secret was that the bulkier top end contrived to fill the space between engine and fuel tank which left none of the gaps that made side-valve bikes looks relatively puny. Instead, the whole bike had the appearance of being packed with machinery – muscle if you like – hunched and ready for action. No wonder the dealers were desperate to sell it.

But of course, being a Harley-Davidson meant that the Knucklehead also came with its quota of birth pangs. The new oil system wasn't perfect, delivering too much oil to some parts of the top end while starving others (the pushrod

tops didn't get any oil supply at all until 1938). Valve springs broke, the early engines drank oil and, as Joe Petrali had warned, they leaked it as well.

There followed the by now familiar ritual of crash engineering programmes, with kits of revised parts being sent out to long-suffering dealers. In fact, nearly 100 modifications were made to the bike in its first year. Luckily, they seemed to do the trick. A change to the pinion gear shaft brought the oil consumption down, and, thanks to a new supplier, the metallurgy of the valve springs was improved. The top end oiling was changed in 1937 too, which overcame most of the problems. But it wasn't until 1941, when a new gear-driven centrifugally-controlled oil pump was introduced, that the Knucklehead's dry sump system finally fulfilled its promise.

Whatever its early problems, the Founders weren't blind to the Knucklehead's potential for speed and glamour which, naturally enough, they calculated would enhance an otherwise dowdy range. In 1937, all the side-valve twins were to get Knucklehead-type styling, and in 1936, the Board authorized Joe Petrali to go for a speed record.

The current measured mile record was 126mph (203km/h) and in a fit of generosity, Walter Davidson promised Petrali a $1,000 bonus if he made 150. The bike certainly looked as if it would deliver. Much attention was paid to streamlining, with aluminium disc-covered wheels and early 1915 forks to keep the frontal area down. With its big tail fairing and elegant blue paint job, the bike looked like a classic Thirties speed machine. They were even going to call it 'Bluebird' until Malcolm Campbell got there first with his record-breaking car.

Despite the oil leaks, the Knucklehead proved surprisingly trouble-free. A tuned version (twin carbs, high compression and higher gearing) captured the mile record at Daytona Beach in 1937.

Right: *A custom bike with a sense of humour? Miami Custom went for a Flintstones theme on this one. Custom bikes in general (and Harleys in particular) are becoming so numerous that a really imaginative paint job is vital if you want to be noticed.*

Opposite: *Owner Arnaldo Gomez has had the engine taken out to 96ci (about 1,600cc) and chromed. The transmission is chromed too, and built by U.S. Steel.*

Mechanically, it was built around a lightweight frame and the bike was tuned up with twin carburettors, magneto ignition, a high lift cam and higher compression. With extra high gearing and high pressure racing tyres, it had a theoretical top whack of 160mph (256km/h). Plenty to clinch the record and just enough for Joe's bonus.

A three-mile course was marked out on Daytona Beach for the inauspicious date of 13 March. The first runs on a tuned 45 brought a disappointing 102.04mph (164.2km/h), but worse was to come. When the Knucklehead first got up to 100mph (160km/h), it began to weave about all over the place. Joe managed to stop it safely, correctly identified the problem and ordered the immediate removal of all aerodynamic aids. Free of the fairings and discs, he went out again, this time clocking up an average 136.18mph (219.1km/h). So the record was won: but it was a rather hollow victory. Not only was it a mere 10mph (16km/h) faster than the old record (set by Johnny Seymour on a 1924 Indian), but Walter Davidson refused Joe his bonus.

Nevertheless, other stunts were to prove the Knucklehead's worth. Maybe after those early debacles Harley-Davidson was particularly keen to prove that its bike was, if not trouble free right from the start, then at least much closer to perfection than it had ever been before. Fred Hamm was a police officer from Pasedena and no stranger to epic rides. In the spring of 1937 he selected a standard 61E and ran it in for 1,200 miles (1,931km) before going for the 24-hour record. A five-mile circle was marked out in the centre of the dry Lake Muroc. Despite sub-zero night-time temperatures and 100°F-plus (40C) conditions during the day, Hamm rode his

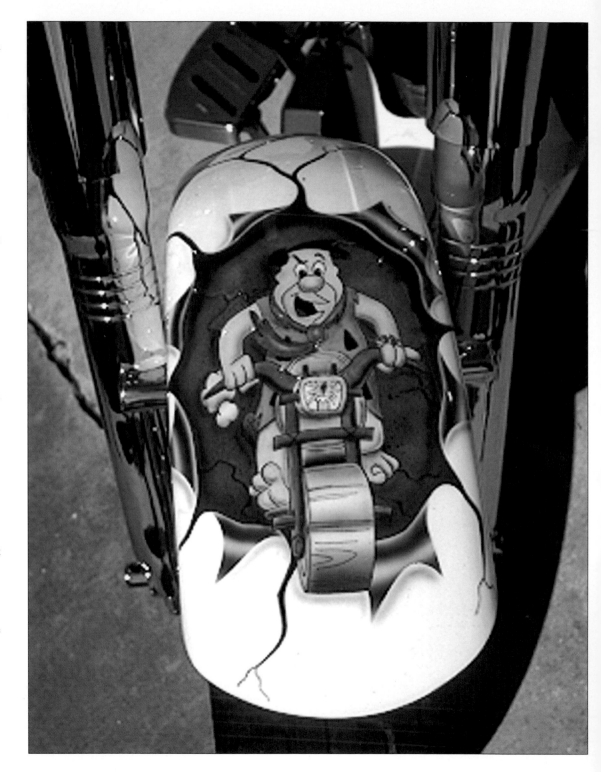

Knucklehead round and round the circle, stopping only for fuel, oil and fruit juice and a single non-scheduled stop for a new rear chain. After 24 hours he had covered 1,825 miles (2937km) at an average 76.02mph (122.3km/h) – forty-three American Motorcycle Association records had been broken.

Feats like this did much to persuade the buying public that this time, Harley really had got it right. Matters were improved still further when the Knucklehead got full valve enclosure in 1938, which helped to keep the oil in and noise down. Of course, it was easier for people to forgive the Knucklehead any early faults because of its looks and power, and it went on selling well.

Harley-Davidson was also learning the value of marketing. Rather than sell accessories *ad hoc*, it began to group them together. The Standard group (an option on all the twins) consisted of a prop stand, Safety Guard (crash bars), a speedometer (with a max-speed-attained hand to prove you weren't bragging), a Ride Control and a steering damper. Or you could really push the boat out and go for the Deluxe group: saddlebags, fender lamp, brake light, rubbers for the foot pedals, dice heads for the switchgear, a dice shift knob (what was it about dice?) and the odd splash of chrome. Still, it worked, for in 1937, 90 per cent of bikes produced were being ordered with one accessories group or the other. Even the police had their own accessory package – siren, speedometer, luggage rack, first-aid kit, fire extinguisher and pursuit lights. That was the Deluxe version – more impoverished forces could order a Standard group which consisted simply of siren and speedo. None of them bothered with the dice heads though.

Accessories regardless, so well was the

Right: *If you're wondering about the setting, it's Daytona Beach where thousands of Harleys, customized or otherwise, congregate during Bike Week.*

Specifications

1936 Knucklehead

Engine	Overhead valve 45-degree V-twin
Bore x stroke	3 $^5/_{16}$ x 3 $^1/_2$ in (84.1 x 88.9 mm)
Capacity	60.3ci (988cc)
Compression ratio	E 6.5:1/E 7.0:1
Power	E 37hp @ 4,800rpm EL 40hp @ 4,800rpm
Gearbox	Four-speed, constant mesh
Clutch	Dry, multiplate
Primary drive	Duplex chain,
Final drive	Chain
Suspension	
Front	Leading link tubular forks
Rear	Rigid
Wheels/tyres	
Front	4.50 x 18
Rear	4.50 x 18
Wheelbase	59 $^1/_2$ in (151cm)
Seat height	26 in (66cm)
Weight	515lb (231kg)
Fuel consumption	35-50mpg (13-18 ltr/km)
Top speed	E 85-90mph (138-145km/h) EL 90-95mph (145-153km/h)

Knucklehead selling by the late Thirties that Bill Harley began to lobby for a smaller version, a 45ci (750cc) ohv bike. He argued that putting an ohv top end onto the existing side-valve bottom end would produce around 30hp. He figured that it should be about as fast as the big 74ci (1200cc)

side-valve and cost about the same to make. Discussion went on at Board level all that year, and the company eventually decided to go ahead with a prototype. It was built, ridden, and showed promise but in the end, Harley-Davidson couldn't bring itself to build a 'baby' 45 that would cost as much as the touring 74. The idea was dropped in 1939, but the 74 ohv did appear. It was almost

identical to the original 61 (1000cc), apart from its engine size. Though Harley-Davidson insisted the idea was to give more torque to sidecar riders, the 74 was appropriately enough welcomed by power-hungry solo riders, too: the Knucklehead had after all started life as Harley's first real sportster.

Left: *You might think that the more elaborate Harley's factory customs became, the less likely riders would be to spend money on changing them. But this 1994 Fat Boy has been given a thorough going over by its owner.*

Chapter Four
Every Dog Has Its Day... The WLA

E very dog has its day, but maybe it's a little unkind to dismiss the ubiquitous WLA's war service quite so readily. After all, nearly 90,000 of the 45ci (750cc) V-twins gave good, reliable service from the frozen Eastern Front to Rommel's 120°F- (50°C-) desert.

While the WLA was undoubtedly slow and heavy, it had the capacity to keep going on minimal maintainance. It was simple enough even for the most cack-handed trooper to fettle and it was economical and easy to ride. In this way, it introduced thousands to motorcycling in general and Harley in particular. Far from putting them off, it whetted many a rider's appetite.

Still, if it hadn't been for the War, there's little doubt that the WLA's reputation would be rather more shaky than it is. Reliable, yes, but overshadowed by more exciting rivals in the Thirties it was condemned to power the three-wheel Servicar for decades after. Instead, the WLA was redeemed by its faithful war service, like some dull but adequate uncle who comes back from war covered in reflected glory.

But war or no war, the WLA's birth was hardly auspicious. The D-series 45 (as it was then known) was part of Harley's 1929 lineup of side-valve blunders which included the underpowered 30ci (500cc) single and troublesome VL. All had their own problems, though the twins at least eventually developed into reliable machines. But the 45 might never have happened at all if Harley-Davidson designer Arthur Constantine hadn't been given the sack (or resigned, depending on whom you believe). In 1925, he had drawn up a unit construction 45ci (750cc) V-twin; Walter Davidson rejected it, and Constantine left to join arch-rival Excelsior. Two years later, out came Excelsior's remarkably similar 45ci Super X,

which was fast (90mph/145km/h) and deservedly popular. Indian, meanwhile, had the Scout 101, another nimble 45ci twin, which wasn't quite as quick as the Super X, but just as popular.

This would never do – Harley-Davidson had to have its own 45ci to meet the opposition head on. The 1929 D-series was the result, but it was hardly the thing to challenge 90-mile-an-hour sportsters. For a start, despite sharing its frame with the 30ci single, this bike was no lightweight at 390lb (177kg). Neither was its long-stroke V-twin over-endowed with power; the basic D could manage only 15hp at 3,900rpm and the high compression DLD an estimated 20hp. Even in that fastest form it could barely broach 70mph (113km/h) and the D was a good 10mph (16km/h) slower. Such were the complaints about the D's performance that dealers were soon supplying performance-boosting kits which included higher compression heads, plus a different carburettor and more favourable gearing.

Even for those happy with its performance, the D wasn't without its teething troubles. Using the single's frame was great for production economics, but the bright spark whose idea it was hadn't noticed that it left nowhere for the V-twin's generator to go. In the end, it had to be mounted vertically alongside the front cylinder. Now this looked distinctly odd, as well as provoking hilarity amongst Indian riders (the first three-cylinder Harley). More seriously, the new generator drive had a tendency to disintegrate under full load. Then there were the 18-inch wheels (the single used 20-inch), which reduced cornering clearance. The gearbox was mounted to the frame rather than the engine, so big torque loadings could sometimes twist engine and box out of alignment. And, unlike the Indian Scout's gear-driven primary

drive, permanently bathed in oil, the D stuck with a chain that had to be oiled by hand periodically. It was also handicapped by its three-speed gearbox, with its massive gap between second and top.

This is all starting to sound like a catalogue of disasters, but it was a testament to the 45's basic strengths (and Harley-Davidson's perseverance) that within a few years the D had developed into a thoroughly reliable, trouble-free two-wheeler. In 1930 it got a new frame and forks which contrived both to lower the seat height and at the same time increase ground clearance. There was more positive lubrication for the primary chain as well, and snazzier colour schemes. A couple of years later, another frame change (a curved downtube) allowed for a horizontal generator, just like those fitted to the big twins; there were aluminium pistons, heavier flywheels and a better oil pump. Now renamed the R-series, the 45 still wasn't fast (a proposed ohv 30ci single was rejected for fear it might embarrass the 45) but most of its early problems were overcome. In 1937 it got the dry-sump oil system which had proved so successful in the Knucklehead and was renamed the W. Meanwhile, the aluminium-headed racers – WR and WLDR – dominated motorcycle racing in the U.S. (if nowhere else), and work progressed on an ohv 45 that promised to outshine Indian on the road as well.

The war put an end to all of that, though the first militarized Ws went, not to the American military, but to Britain. England's Midlands, where Triumphs and BSAs were churned out by the thousand, was the Luftwaffe's first target in 1940. The motorcycle factories in Coventry and Birmingham were obliterated, so Harley and Indian suddenly found themselves exporting bikes equipped for wartime use.

Opposite: *The WL was Harley's answer to the Indian Sport Scout and Excelsior Super X. It was no match for these nimble 45s, but it carved its own niche in the Servicar and wartime WLA markets.*

Right: War service may have been the side-valve 45's finest hour, but it was to survive a great deal longer, powering utilities and Servicars for the police into the 1970s.

Things had moved on since the First World War, when it was enough to paint a bike in drab olive before sending it to the Front: but the WLA was very different to its civilian counterpart. The engine was naturally the lowest compression version available, with enlarged cooling fins to enable it to cope with first-gear slogs across country. Eighteen-inch wheels and big D-section mudguards helped prevent mud clogging off-road, and there was a substantial skidplate to protect the engine and gearbox. A big oil-bath air cleaner was added, along with a heavy duty luggage rack, ammo boxes and rifle scabbard. All this, of course, added to the WLA's weight, which implies that a militarized WL should have been even more sluggardly than the basic version, though it depends on who you believe. According to Harry Sucher in *The Milwaukee Marvel,* the bike could only just top 50mph (80km/h), but prototype WLAs (the 'A' was for Army) reportedly managed 65mph (105km/h) in U.S. Army tests. Still, unless one was being pursued by the BMW-mounted Wehrmacht, it was all rather academic – the 45 was reliable, which counted for rather more than top speed out in the field.

Five thousand militarised WLs were sent to Britain early in the war, but it soon became clear that far bigger contracts were around the corner. For the first eighteen months of war, the U.S. was no more than an Allied sympathizer, but everything changed after Pearl Harbor. As solos, WLAs were used to relay messages (useful when radio silence was imposed) or patrol difficult terrain. With sidecar and machine gun attached, the motorcycle became a highly manoeuvrable combat vehicle, but once again the U.S. Army needed a standard motorcycle.

Straightaway, tests began at Fort Knox. The prototype WLA was compared to a Delco (basically the same as a pre-war BMW) and a 30ci (500cc) twin from Indian. The tests weren't always very scientific – the overheating test consisted of riding the bikes around very slowly, then placing a hand on the engine; but the WLA's big-finned engine stood it in good stead. It did well on the fording test (a depth of 16 in/41cm), too. Harley-Davidson simply pointed the oil breather tube upwards, which prevented water from getting sucked into the crankcase: the bike proved less susceptible to mud-clogging than either the Indian or the Delco.

Despite the inspectors' reservations (they thought the WLA was rather too heavy, would have preferred shaft drive and didn't like its inability to keep water out of the primary drive) Harley-Davidson got its big contract in January 1942. Indian got one as well, but by now Harley was by far the bigger of the two. The first contract was for just over 30,000 machines, to be delivered by the end of 1943. In the event, nearly three times that number were built by the end of the war, and the WLA accounted for the vast majority of Harley-Davidson's wartime production. That was despite a number of alternative projects (some would say blind alleys) which came to nothing. These were usually inspired by the military itself, who couldn't believe that a 14-year-old civilian design could be equal to the rigours of modern warfare. But, apart from the inevitable chain wear problems in Saharan sands, it was.

Engaged on priority war work, Harley-Davidson now had the authority to procure all the aluminum, rubber and steel it needed to make motorcycles. Yet there were still some shortages,

and the Army requested that all unnecessary rubber be left off the WLAs – rubber footrests and kickstarter pedals were out. Chrome was left off as well, which at least went part way to answering the Army's beef about WLA's weight.

In fact, the WLA was far from ideal from the Army's point of view: the military really wanted shaft drive (with the desert war in mind) and they thought 750cc was excessive for such a low-powered machine. The British were after all making do with 350/500cc singles, and officials pressured William Harley to make a smaller 30ci twin. One was reputed to have said, 'If you don't make that 30 cubic inch motor for us, you can

consider yourselves out of the motorcycle business.' Fortunately, Bill refused, and the Army eventually became convinced that 45ci was fine – it wasn't too bad on fuel (35-37mpg/13 ltr/km) and being a big engine, it was nicely understressed.

There were of course one or two variations on the WL theme. WLC was for the Canadian forces (Canada had been in the war since 1939) and, although mechanically similar to the WLA, it differed from it in several ways. It used the big twin's forks and front brake, transposed the clutch and front brake levers and had a foot gearchange. It didn't have the WLA's rear luggage rack

(designed for a 40lb/18kg radio) but countered with a toolbox on the front mudguard. Twenty thousand of them were built, so the WLC formed a substantial part of Harley's wartime output.

But the U.S. Army still wanted (or thought it wanted) a shaft-drive flat twin as its standardized military motorcycle; in other words, an Americanized BMW. Harley and Indian were invited to bid for an initial run of 1,000 bikes, which, if all went well, would lead to an order for 25,000. Indian came up with the 841, a Moto-Guzzi style transverse V-twin, but William Harley took the idea to its logical conclusion. He somehow procured a genuine BMW from Europe

and had the Milwaukee Design Department convert all its millimetres to inches!

The resulting XA was a 750cc side-valve flat twin, with very little to distinguish it from its Bavarian progenitor. The army testers loved it – the XA ran cooler than the WLA did without its messy chain drive and went further between overhauls. On the other hand, it was expensive – Harley-Davidson charged the Government $1,000 for each of the 1,000 XAs, and even then William H. Davidson was to complain that it was virtually given away. The XA also used a lot of precious aluminium (65lb/29kg of it, where the WLA used only 45lb/20kg). Still, it was all a moot point, as the Jeep came along to take over the role of these more sophisticated bikes, and the desert war for which the XA was intended had already been won. So it was dropped. There were plans for a post-war civilian version, with overhead valves and telescopic forks, but they came to nothing and neither did wartime schemes for an XA-powered two-wheel-drive sidecar outfit. There were also plans for an Allis-Chalmers XA powered snow sled, a mini-Jeep (using a bigger 49ci/800cc ohv XA) and a generator set. The XA was even mooted as the possible basis for an updated shaft-drive Servicar – there seemed no end to its uses. Unfortunately, the war's end really did put a stop to all these initiatives and by the late Forties Harley-Davidson was more concerned with churning out what it knew would sell: V-twins.

But did the company have a good war? While Harley-Davidson got plenty of business from the Government and was able to expand, it certainly did not make its fortune. The WLAs were supplied on a cost-plus 10 per cent basis, so the profit margins weren't massive. True, there was a big order for spares as well – Harley produced enough of them to remake another 30,000 WLAs – but it got no compensation for the massive overstocks left when the war ended. For years afterwards, all over the world, brand-new unused WLAs, their engine units and all manner of bits and pieces, went on sale at rock bottom prices. But publicity is a valuable thing, and all these ex-army Harleys brought thousands of people into Harley-Davidson ownership. Even more importantly for the civilian market, many of the returning GIs found that the experience of riding a Harley-Davidson was one of their more pleasant wartime memories and went on to buy a

Specifications
1942 WLA

Engine	Side valve 45-degree V-twin
Bore x stroke	$2^{3/4}$ x $3^{13/16}$in (69.9 x 107.4mm)
Capacity	45.12ci (750cc)
Compression ratio	5.0:1
Power	23bhp @ 4,600rpm
Torque	28lb ft @ 3,000rpm
Gearbox	Three-speed, constant mesh, hand change
Gear ratios	1st:11.71:1 2nd:7.45:1 3rd:4.74:1
Clutch	Dry, single plate
Primary drive	Duplex chain,
Final drive	Chain
Suspension	
Front	Leading-link forks
Rear	None
Wheels/tyres	
Standard	4.00 x 18in
Desert	5.50 x 18in
Wheelbase	$57^{1/2}$in (146cm)
Seat height	32in (81cm)
Weight	576lb (261kg)
Ground clearance	4in (102mm)
Fuel capacity	$3^{3/8}$ gallons (16 litres)
Fuel consumption	37 mpg (13 ltr/km) est.
Cruising range	125 miles (200km) est.
Maximum gradient	30%
Top speed	65mph (105km/h)

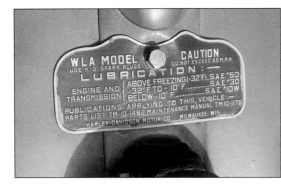

big twin for themselves. As for the 45, the sow's ear may not have become a silk purse, but it had developed into a thoroughly dependable hog.

Chapter Five
Keeping the Faith: The Panhead

Look at the Duo Glide pictured here. Big, fat and heavy, it looks little different to the first Knucklehead of 1936, or indeed any other big touring Harley before or since. So did it deserve some of the less complimentary road tests of the time, which castigated it as an outdated dinosaur, lumbering towards its inevitable demise at the hands of younger, nimbler rivals? As so often in history, the answer is yes, and no.

It's true that next to any Triumph, Norton or BSA you cared to compare it with, the Duo Glide was a ponderous thing, with clunky, heavyweight controls and a ground-scraping undercarriage that discouraged hard cornering. Just look at the figures – a 1949 Panhead had 50hp and a contemporary Triumph Thunderbird 42hp. But the Triumph weighed less than 400lb (181kg) and the Harley nearly 700 (318kg). It could also offer a slick-shifting, foot-change gearbox, nimble handling and could touch 100mph (160km/h) – the Panhead had none of this.

British bikes like that Triumph transformed the American motorcycle market in the 1950s, just as the Japanese were to do in the following decade. Triumph and the rest would in their turn be seen as outdated crudities as many riders regarded Harley-Davidson in those post-war years – 'Hawg' became a term of abuse. So it was little wonder that by the mid-Sixties, Harley's share of the home market had shrunk to about five per cent. It must have seemed like a cruel twist of fate to Harley-Davidson, which in 1953 had finally seen Indian fall by the wayside to give it its long-desired monopoly of the traditional bike market.

All of this is true. And yet it's unfair to deride the Harleys of the time as simply outdated. All the major updates of the period – hydraulic forks, swinging-arm rear suspension, alloy cylinder heads, even electric start – came at around the same time the imported bikes were beginning to offer them or even, in the case of the electric start, beforehand. Neither was it the case that the market for big, heavy tourers had been overtaken by events. It was still there, but it had become a niche market. And there were still committed tourists who would consider nothing but a Harley. Bikes like these might well be irrelevant in Britain or Europe, where roads were more narrow and twisty and the towns closer together. For an Englishman ear-'oling his way through the circuitous Cat & Fiddle Pass between Buxton and Macclesfield, an FLH Harley was a joke. But as *Cycle World* put it at the time, an FLH Harley provided the man setting out from Fairbanks and heading for Miami his best chance of getting there without incident. The point was that the motorcycle market was becoming more compartmentalized; the touring niche was still very much alive, and Harley-Davidson was serving it with gradually updated machines.

Things were different just after the War. The Marshall Plan, a massive American-funded foreign aid programme designed to help get the war-ravaged bits of Europe back on their industrial feet, meant fewer resources for American manufacturers – the British bike makers had their supplies of steel and aluminium rationed as did Harley. So exotic new models were out, and the pre-war line of side-valve 45s and 74s (750 and 1200cc), plus Knucklehead 61s (1000cc) and 74s, trickled back into production. As it happened, the side-valves soon got relegated into special orders only (it was said that

South American police orders for the 74 side-valve were all that kept it going in its last few years) and they disappeared altogether in 1951-2. But the ohv big twins continued to be the mainstay of Harley-Davidson's production, and they've stayed that way ever since.

Not that there was ever any room for complacency. The Knucklehead might have been a great leap forward when it was announced a decade before, but times were changing. Just as smoother, better roads and better fuels had made the Knucklehead possible in the Thirties, so now in its turn, they made it obsolete. The main problem was its cast-iron cylinder heads – they were easy and cheap to make, with no need for valve-seat inserts, but they weren't so good at dissipating heat. As roads got straighter, so bikes ran faster and were more likely to overheat – the Knucklehead did, with all the attendant pre-ignition and valve problems.

Harley-Davidson's answer was simple: cast the heads in aluminium alloy, which has three times the heat conductivity of iron. The result was undoubtedly more complex and expensive to make – there were aluminium-bronze valve seat inserts and the valves ran in steel guides. The rocker arm support came in two parts: cast-iron lower and bronze upper, and there had to be steel inserts for the head bolts and spark plugs as well (anyone who has stripped an alloy plug thread will know why). But it was all worth it. Harley took the opportunity to build in a shallower valve angle of 78.5°, which allowed a decent compression ratio without having to resort to excessively domed pistons. Less combustion-chamber area meant reduced heat-flow into the valve gear.

But perhaps more significant was the

At a quick glance, this 1950 EL Panhead looks like a sensitively restored example. Wrong: the frame was built in 1995 by Paugcho and is fitted with Wide Glide forks; neither did 1950 Harleys come in Wineberry/Gold and White Pearl with gold tint.

introduction of hydraulic tappets. Using these on the Panhead was really making a virtue of necessity. Aluminium expands more rapidly with heat than does iron, and hydraulic tappets offered a means of keeping valve clearances consistent, whatever the engine's temperature. Not only that, they promised to eliminate tappet noise and the tiresome ritual of valve setting, such a necessary part of life for anyone maintaining a pushrod engine.

The new top end was finished off with big pan-shaped rocker covers (hence 'Panhead') which gave the engine a much cleaner appearance, a look that was underlined by routing the oil lines through the inside of the engine. A larger oil pump was claimed to deliver 25 per cent more oil to the rockers than before,

and there was a new camshaft and new manifolds as well. The Panhead gave around 50hp at 4,800rpm and weighed 8lb (4kg) less than its predecessor, though that wasn't a huge saving on a machine weighing 600lb (272kg).

It all looked like a real advance, and it was; the Panhead ran faster and cooler than the Knucklehead and it was a genuine step forward in the V-twin's story. Still, it wouldn't have been a real Harley without some teething troubles, and the Pan duly obliged. Those hidden oilways did make the engine much neater and less likely to leak, but they were a positive labyrinth through which even the uprated pump, located as it was low down in the bowels of the engine, found it difficult to force oil. The result was fluctuating oil pressure, which upset the hydraulic tappets,

which in turn did the valve timing no good at all. In some cases, rocker arms snapped and in time honoured fashion, Harley-Davidson was reduced to hurriedly sending fix-up kits of new parts out to the dealers.

The solution, which Harley-Davidson took five years to reach, was to move the hydraulic tappets from the top to the base of the pushrods. At least now if pressure surges did occur, they would affect the valve timing proportionately less. The only other Panhead problem of any note was the infamous felt pad, which was stuck to the underside of the rocker cover. The commendably simple purpose of this pad was to catch oil splashes and thus allow them to drip back down onto the valvegear. This it did until DIY mechanics ripped the pads out, thinking

they had been mistakenly left there by the factory. It was only when everything was screwed back together again that the pads' secondary role became obvious – they damped out the otherwise clattery top end noise.

Despite the problems (which by Harley-Davidson's track record standards, were relatively minor) few would argue that the Panhead was overall A Good Thing. But eyebrows were raised when in 1949 the bike gained telescopic front forks. It wasn't that they were particularly high tech or new-fangled (most British bikes had adopted them, or were about to), but they were different: they spelt the end of the leading-link springer forks which Harley-Davidson had used for over forty years: the original designs that Bill Harley come up with at college. Shocked enthusiasts might have been mollified had they known that, another forty years on, springer forks would return as part of Harley-Davidson's ongoing nostalgia trip.

As ever, this latest product of the Harley-Davidson's Design Department wasn't flawless. The early vented versions had a habit of spraying the rider with oil, and their long travel could allow the bike to dig into the ground on tight turns. Diehard riders complained that the new forks robbed the bike of its low-speed steering precision as well. Overall though, the new forks were good news, giving unprecedented comfort in conjunction with the big, soft rear tyre and the sprung saddle, all serving to underline the Panhead's role as the tourists' machine. A Norton might be quicker on short trips, but the rider wouldn't be as happy after 300 miles (483km). The new forks also brought about a piece of Harley-Davidson history trivia – the bike was named 'Hydra-Glide', the first V-twin to be

Left: *This bike is just as it would have left the factory thirty-six years ago, and it has covered only 23,500 miles (nearly 38,000km) since then.*

Opposite: *A 1960 FL, resplendent in Hi-Fi Blue and White with whitewall tyres and kitted out for touring with the 'King of the Highway' option pack.*

blessed with an official factory name rather than just a number. The Hydra-Glide soon gained a foot gearchange as well, but you could insist on laughing in the face of progress if you wished by opting for the good old handchange instead, which remained an option.

So comfortable was the Hydra-Glide that many committed Harley riders would look down at the effete swinging-arm rear suspension some of the British bikes were beginning to use, despite the even greater comfort, not to mention better handling on bumpy corners, it offered. Fortunately, Milwaukee knew better than to ignore the march of progress completely, and 1958 saw its own version of a swinging-arm rear end. This was a feature of the Duo Glide and it represented another step in the slow evolution of the big touring Harley. Here again, additional weight and mechanical complexity was probably a price worth paying for the extra comfort and surer handling offered.

Still, there was plenty of resistance to the change, even among the police. The California Highway Patrol ordered new Duo Glides, only to complain of instability at high speeds. The officers blamed the new rear suspension and wanted that nice simple, rigid rear end back again. John Nowak, Dean of the company's Service School, made the journey westward to investigate and found that the instability had nothing to do with the new rear suspension – someone had set up the steering-head bearings too tight. There was, however, a genuine problem with the Duo Glide front forks. Despite (according to David Wright) the fact that prototypes had been running around from as early as 1948, it was later found that the fork seals on the Duo Glide were rubbing its fork legs to a mirror finish. The resulting tolerance was so tight that it wouldn't let any oil through at all. Looser tolerance seals, and a rougher finish for the fork legs, solved that one.

In fact, as the Fifties gave way to the Sixties, the Duo Glide (which still came in low compression FL and high compression FLH forms) had developed into a well integrated machine, for its intended purpose at least. It was as though, having first sorted out the engine, Harley-Davidson could then concentrate on keeping the rest of the bike up to date, which is exactly what it did. The hand gearchange/foot clutch was relegated to the options list back in 1952, while the full suspension and massive saddle made the Duo just right for long trips: Harley-Davidson electrics had long been reliable and trouble-free. None of this meant that the Duo Glide was ever likely to win conquest sales from riders who had started out on a Triumph or (increasingly) a Honda. For them, the Harley was something that rumbled slowly along the straights, wallowed round corners and needed a superman to lift it if, Lord forbid, it ever fell over.

But for its intended market, the Duo Glide reflected what was about right. It reflected the American 'dresser' tradition which has never caught on in Europe in quite the same way. This movement originated in the 1920s, when touring clubs began to dress up their Harley-Davidsons or Indians in the same sort of touring regalia. Leather panniers were a must, and screens, spotlights and fairings soon followed. All across the States, clubs sprang up that catered exclusively for tourists such as the all-women Motor Maids, for example, founded by Virna Griffith in the Thirties, and countless others. Many had strict dress codes, with militaristic caps, breeches and boots that would now look slightly comical. But at the time, it was all part of the disciplined, clean-cut image that the American Motorcycle Association was trying hard to portray. In the end, the events at Hollister (a hyped-up 'riot' which cast outlaw bikers as the villains) and films like *The Wild One* put paid to that, though the niche for the traditional touring V-twin carried on regardless.

Cycle World tested a Duo Glide in 1964 and were surprisingly complimentary. By this time, the Panhead was producing 60hp, enough for a 15.8 second standing quarter-mile time and a very theoretical 129mph (208km/h) maximum (97mph/156km/h), in practice). More to the point, for its intended use the Duo could be stuck into its long-striding top gear as soon as you liked. You could then use the torque to accelerate seamlessly from 15mph (24km/h) up to about 80 (129km/h). So it was a pity that the tester found that at a typical 65-70mph (105-113km/h) cruising speed, the wind and vibration tried to push the rider's feet off the rests, that a gear change resulted in a 'pronounced clank', and that the front brake was 'largely ineffectual' for emergency stops. Naturally, the bike proved to be as stable as the Rock of Gibraltar regardless of side winds and bad roads; it could carry huge loads without suffering significant losses in performance; and it 'rides extremely smoothly', so persevering with the suspension had been worthwhile after all. It wasn't a cheap means of transport any more, gobbling fuel at 30mpg (11 ltr/km), and costing more to buy than almost any other bike. Consequently, there were lots of riders who would never consider one, just as many Harley-Davidson owners would countenance no other. But then that's just what happened to Harley's Big Twin after the war – it changed from a mainstream to a niche product.

Specifications
1964 Duo Glide FLH

Engine	OHV, 45-degree V-twin
Bore x stroke	3.44in x 3.97in (87.4 x 100.8mm)
Capacity	73.7ci (1207cc)
Compression ratio	8.0:1
Carburettor	Linkert 1.5 in, M-74-B
Ignition	Battery and coil
Power	60bhp @ 5,400rpm
Gearbox	Four-speed, constant mesh
Gear ratios	1st:11.2:1 2nd:6.79:1 3rd:4.58:1 4th:3.73:1
Clutch	Dry, multi-plate
Primary drive	Duplex chain,
Final drive	Chain
Suspension	
Front	Telescopic forks
Rear	Swinging arm
Brakes	
Front	Drum, cable operated
Rear	Drum, hydraulic
Wheels/tyres	
Standard	5.00 x 16in
Desert	5.00 x 16in
Wheelbase	61¹⁄₂ in (155cm)
Seat height	30 in (76cm)
Weight	690lb (313kg)
Fuel capacity	3 ³⁄₄ gallons (US)
Fuel consumption	30 mpg (11 ltr/km) est.
Cruising range	125 miles (198km)
Top speed	97 mph (156km/h)

Left: *The Electra Glide must be the best known Harley name of all time. Born in 1965 (the Panhead's final year), it lived on as a Shovelhead and is still the top of the Evolution range.*

Left: *When photographed in the early 1990s, this Electra Glide had covered only 28,000 miles (45,000km) from new. At that rate, it should rumble past the 100,000 (160,000) mark in about 2068.*

Chapter Six
Racers: The
Accidental Heroes

Right: *If XR fanciers hadn't
realized before getting this close,
the single carburettor would give
the game away – all XR750s had
twin carburettors.*

Opposite: *It looks like an XR750
in its classic red and black livery.
The frame is XR, but the engine
is from a road-going 54ci (883cc)
Sportster. Genuine XR engines
were Sportster-derived but
de-stroked to get them under the
45ci (750cc) C Class limit.*

They never wanted to race at all, Harley and the Davidsons. As we've seen, they simply weren't interested in making the sort of bike that would win races. Actually that isn't quite true, for they did want to build a bike that ran and kept running. In early competition, endurance mattered far more than mere speed.

But in those days, the Founders saw racing purely as a means of proving reliability – not for them was the shallow glory of coming first for its own sake. Perhaps that was partly why the factory's involvement with racing was a little sporadic, at least before the Second World War. Fortunately, there were generations of tuners, riders and enthusiastic owners who just went out there and did it: whether the factory was involved or not, Harley-Davidson rapidly became a major force in racing.

Walter Davidson was actually the first Harley-Davidson factory rider. The Founders had done their best to ignore competition for the first few years, but by 1908, seeing how rivals were able to make useful propganda out of winning, they decided to give it a go. Walter shipped a standard 5/35 single to New York for the first big endurance 'race' (it was more of a time trial) to be held in the U.S. The two-day event commenced at dawn on 29 June in Catskill. Half the field had fallen by the wayside by the time the survivors reached Brooklyn that night, but Walter was still in the running. Next day there was a 180-mile (290-km) circuit of Long Island, which Walter completed by arriving at each checkpoint bang on time. When the scores were totted up, he was the only rider to have a perfect 1,000 point record. Needless to say, he won. And the following week, still on Long Island, he managed an amazing 188mpg (67 ltr/km) in a

hilly economy run – another victory. The year after, Harley-Davidson snatched the Team Prize in another endurance run this time, from Cleveland to Indianapolis.

But the nature of motorcycle sport in America was changing from endurance time-trials for what were basically standard bikes to proper racing, either on county horse-tracks or purpose-built 'motordromes'. The horse-tracks in particular led to that peculiarly American sport of dirt racing. A regular feature at county fairs, dirt racing has always been the heart of the sport – hillclimbs and drag racing have had their adherents, but much of Harley's competition history comes from the flat track events. It's only relatively recently that circuit racing has come onto the scene, so naturally enough, American racing bikes have developed in a particular way – brakes and suspension and handling finesse didn't matter as much as sheer power.

This was the background to Harley's first purpose-built racer, the Model 17 eight-valve V-twin. William Ottaway (a leading light in Harley-Davidson's early engineering history) had been busy upgrading the F-model ioe twins, but as average speeds around the oval race tracks crept up to 80mph (129km), then 90mph, it became obvious that something special was needed. The Model 17 actually wasn't quite as original as it's sometimes given credit for – crankcases and flywheels were pure F-model and even the bore/stroke (and therefore the 61ci (1000cc) capacity) were the same. It was the top end of the engine that made it special. Carl Hedstrom at Indian had already graphically demonstrated that four overhead valves offered far better breathing than anything else, so that's what the 17 had.

Unfortunately, the first prototypes were a classic example of practice not measuring up to theory. Although strongly influenced by the work of Harry Ricardo, the new bikes suffered from pre-ignition and tended to eat spark plugs. It was with some difficulty that Ottaway persuaded the careful Walter Davidson to pay for Ricardo himself to cross the Atlantic and sort out the engine for the company. It was worth it, as the Englishman had the problems ironed out within weeks and Harley-Davidson had a top ranking competition V-twin reliably producing 55hp.

The engine was fitted to a typical flat-track frame (actually the earlier II-K frame, but slightly longer and with more rake in the forks); being a dirt racer, the Model 17 had no brakes. This was a lot safer than it sounded, as on the oval flat tracks, riders had no 90-degree S-bends to negotiate – they simply tore down the straight then slid around the bends speedway style. No brakes meant no sudden stops, and there were few rear-end collisions in dirt racing. Which was just as well, as the eight-valve was a near-120mph (193km/h) machine and the only way of stopping it was to flick the magneto cut-out switch. It also had direct drive (no clutch, one gear) and very high compression, so starting, as well as stopping, needed a certain knack. You held the valve lifter on, got a push from two or three strong men or (preferably) a tow by car; you then dropped the lifter once you were up to speed – and you were off.

In theory, you could buy an eight-valve for $1,500, but when the equivalent Indian racer cost a mere $350 it was obvious that Harley-Davidson didn't see this as a cheap bike for privateers. The company wasn't yet at the stage of subsidizing private racers. Whether the 17 was worth that much more than an Indian is a moot point, but it

did bring Harley a string of competition successes. Racers like 'Red' Parkhurst and Otto Walker (the official Harley-Davidson team was soon known as the Wrecking Crew) virtually swept the board in 1916, and did it again three years later. Alas, the expense was too much for the Founders to swallow. The Wrecking Crew was disbanded in 1922 and in future Harley's 'official' racers were developed from their road bikes. The eight-valve's reign was brief, but at least it showed Harley-Davidson that racing was worthwhile.

If the eight-valve was an exotic racer, the WR was anything but. Between the wars, racing had become the preserve of bikes like the eight-valve – expensive factory specials which were way out of the weekend racer's reach. Things had previously been somewhat more balanced by the fact that earlier racing bikes were often based on Harley's 45 side-valve. The 45 was a sluggardly thing, but it had price and availability on its side. So when the American Motorcycling Association (by this time entirely dependent on Harley-Davidson and Indian) set up a new Class C for production racing, the WR was the natural result: a racier development of the 45. According to the new rules, anything in Class C had to be just as it left the factory – you could remove lights, brakes and licence plate, but that was it. Of course, as ever with production racing, if the factory chose to make something designed to win races, and made several hundred of them, well, that was a production bike, wasn't it?

It was allegedly the same WR as those versions which, despite lacking the stronger, lighter, frames of their counterparts, were certainly on sale in any Harley dealership. It also had alloy heads with larger valves and ports than

ohv advantage. Compare the typical Harley flat-tracker, with its rigid rear end, limited-travel forks and cumbersome hand gearchange controlling a wide ratio three-speed gearbox to, say, a Norton International – sprung frame, 500cc ohc single, foot change, four-speed close ratios. Years ahead of the Harley, in other words. To put it bluntly, the American racing bike of the 1930s, boxed into its dirt track dominated home ground, had fallen behind developments in international competition. Given this, it's difficult to see the Class C rules as anything but an attempt to postpone the inevitable.

No account of Harley-Davidson's competition history, however brief, would be complete without mention of Joe Petrali. As well as being a supremely gifted rider, he was for a

Left: *Unlike some of its dirt-track predecessors, the XR750 has had to adapt itself to circuit racing as well.*

Below: *Micah Stevenson of Fort Worth, Texas, powers his 1972 XR750 around one of Daytona's curves.*

the standard version, and high-lift cams. If you wanted to tailor your WR to a particular course or type of racing, there were countless different gears, sprockets, wheels and tanks on offer as options to suit. The WR really played the same role as the BSA Gold Star did in Britain – it was adaptable enough to be used for different types of competition, cheap enough for weekend racers to buy, and theoretically capable of being ridden to work during the week as well – though this of course excluded those rather special WRs that had to be towed to race meetings. But although it was a very different bike to the WL, the WR was still within the spirit of the original aims of Class C; to make racing

affordable again.

There was another, more controversial side to the WR and the class it raced in. From the start, Class C was open to 45ci (750cc) side-valve bikes and to 30ci (500cc) ohvs (i.e. to the imports). Now there were, and are, those who said that this was all a ruse to keep British twins out of the running. Allan Girdler, on the other hand, in his book *Harley-Davidson: The American Motorcycle,* maintains that the rules were fair and that they allowed open racing for different machines. But while the capacity difference was understandable, there were also restrictions on compression ratio, which prevented the imports from using their natural

number of years Harley-Davidson's one-man competition team, keeping up an official presence in hard times when the factory would no doubt have preferred to abandon the expensive business of racing altogether.

Born in San Francisco of Italian parents, his good fortune started at the age of two – his parents moved to Sacramento just days before the 1906 earthquake. Joe's natural talent for things mechanical soon emerged. He had his first bike at thirteen, was winning board-track races at sixteen and worked as a mechanic at an Indian dealer in between times. Factory rides with Indian followed until 1925, when chance gave him the last-minute loan of a Harley-Davidson factory bike at the Altoona board track. In fairy-tale fashion, he blew the opposition away at an average 100mph (160km/h), then immediately left for home, leaving Harley officials searching for the mystery rider who they were anxious to sign up.

They found him eventually, and Joe went on to dominate the 21ci (350cc) class on a C single – he won every single national event in 1935 and was an excellent hillclimb rider as well. His development expertise showed up in the design of the road going Knucklehead and (always the sign of a good rider) he had few accidents. After retiring from racing in 1938 he worked for Howard Hughes, acting as engineer on the one and only flight of the infamous Spruce Goose. This talented man died of natural causes in 1972.

Joe Petrali no doubt looked at the development of competition Harleys with wry amusement. While developing the Knucklehead in the mid-1930s he had urged Walter Davidson to sanction an ohv 45ci (750cc) bike as well. This would outperform the Indian Sport Scout on both road and track and Bill Harley was to press for the same thing a few years later.

But not only did Harley-Davidson stick with side-valves for the WR racer, it did the same with the KR which replaced the W in 1952. Of course, by this time there was some credible ohv opposition to face up to, so maybe there was less reason to go ohv than there had been before the war. Like the WR, the KR production racer was based on the equivalent road going 45ci side-valve. In this case, it was the K-series, an odd mixture of ancient and modern, which was Harley-Davidson's answer to Norton and all the other nimble imports. It married thoroughly modern running gear (telescopic forks, swinging-arm frame, foot change, unit-construction gearbox) with a side-valve engine.

Now just how closely this side-valve was related to the ancient W-series is a matter of contention. It was a 45-degree V-twin with the same bore and stroke as the W. Some say it was simply a development of the old unit, others that it was all-new. Whatever, it was still outmoded and its 38bhp in 1952 simply wasn't enough. Still, it was also a triumph of development over design, and by the late Sixties the factory and various privateers had coaxed it up to over 60bhp.

It was still winning races then as well, at least on the flat-tracks. In fact, it dominated flat-track racing for nearly two decades. In eighteen seasons of racing, imports won the national championship five times, but KR-mounted riders snatched the other thirteen. And they weren't all on factory specials either: private KR riders actually came first more often than the factory backed team did. As with the WR, there was a whole generation of tuners – Tom Sifton is just one example – who had intricate knowledge of how to get the best out of a side-valve engine. All KRs had their valve train inclined slightly in order to make the side-valves at least a little less

Left: *The KR-series was Harley Davidson's standard racing bike for nearly twenty years, but even when it was introduced, its side-valve engine looked outmoded against its European opposition. This 1953 KR, is owned by John Cygnor.*

Opposite: *Specialist race series, like the Battle of the Twins, BEARS (British, European, American) and 883 Sportster racing have enabled Harley to stay on track outside the U.S.*

restricting than they would otherwise have been, while the factory was willing to sell parts and dispense advice. But beyond that, the way to win was to use all those years of experience to make incremental changes. Nearly everyone used KRs anyway, so the smallest advantage could mean the difference between winning and losing.

Some of this homespun wisdom had less credibility. Dirt-track racers often discarded the KR's modern swinging arm for a special bolt-on rigid rear end. This hardtail (years before customizers made it fashionable) came out of the notion that too much suspension was a bad idea – it was thought that valuable power was used up in compressing it and that it actually reduced traction on smooth surfaces. Well, maybe, but it's worth noting that the XR750 which replaced the KR kept its swinging arm intact, even when dirt racing.

The KR's reign finally came to an end in 1970, when the American Motorcycle Association changed the Class C rules to allow 750cc ohv and overhead cam engines. This naturally gave free rein to the British and the Japanese; Harley's XR750 was Milwaukee's (successful) answer to this new challenge. It's a bit of a chicken and egg situation though – were the rules changed because the XR750 was ready, or was the bike a hurried response to the rule change? Allan Girdler reckons that British interests in the American Motorcycle Association pushed the changes through. If you believe Harry Sucher, Harley-Davidson waited until its XR750 was ready before instructing a compliant American Motorcycle Association to make the changes that suited it.

Whichever, the XR750 at first did not cover itself in glory. The early bikes were heavy and

underpowered and in both 1970 and 1971 the national championship went to BSA/Triumph as a result. It wasn't until aluminium cylinder heads and barrels had been developed and made reliable that the XR took over the traditional Harley-Davidson role of dominating U.S. flat-track racing. Like every competition Harley, the XR wasn't all-new. The double-loop frame was very close to that of the later KRs, while the ohv V-twin was basically the Sportster engine, destroked to get it within the 45ci/750cc class limit.

It wasn't quite as simple as that though; as the XR developed, it moved further and further away from its XL Sportster roots. No other

Harley has oversquare bore/stroke dimensions, or for that matter twin Mikuni carburettors, twin plug heads or self-aligning main bearings. And like the KR, the XR has been subjected to that same endless, year-on-year development programme. In 1970, the XR produced 62bhp at 6,200rpm, with a broad power band starting at 4,800rpm. By the late Eighties it was up to 90bhp and it develops over 100bhp.

While Harley's flat-track rivals – Indian, Triumph and the rest – have fallen by the wayside, the XR has kept going and kept winning. It's interesting to note that when Honda finally beat Harley-Davidson on the track, it was with an updated version of the XR pattern. Like

Right: *The XR750TT performed a similar function on twisty tarmac circuits to the earlier KR-TT. This 1972 version is a replica of a bike owned by Mark Brelsford.*

Opposite: *Owner Keith Campbell puts his XR through its paces around Daytona's infield.*

the WR and KR, the XR750 is a product of its environment. Incremental changes to a tried and tested design are what make it so durably competitive: the Founders would have approved.

Specifications
XR 750

Engine	OHV, 45-degree V-twin
Bore x stroke	3.12in x 2.98in (79.4 x 75.8mm)
Capacity	45ci (750cc)
Compression ratio	10.5:1
Carburettors	2 x 36mm Mikunis
Ignition	Electronic, twin plugs
Power	c.100 bhp
Gearbox	Four-speed, constant mesh
Clutch	Dry, multi-plate
Primary drive	Triplex chain,
Final drive	Chain
Suspension	
Front	Telescopic forks
Rear	Swinging arm, twin dampers
Wheels/tyres	4.00 x 19in
Weight	290lb (132kg)

Chapter Seven
The Sportster: Back in Contention

Right: *What made the Sportster a success was its overhead valves though, if the Harley Board had listened to Joe Petrali, a Sportster could have been on sale in 1939.*

Opposite: *The 1957 Sportster, the first of the line. It was the first Harley-Davidson light enough to compete with the British imports in a straight-line contest. Despite that, it would always be the 'baby Harley' as far as the Big Twin riders were concerned.*

Sportster – the bike that put Milwaukee back in contention with imported road burners. Yet it's the bike that, left to itself, Harley-Davidson would probably never have made.

It's often said that there are three groups of riders within the Harley-Davidson community: touring, custom and sport. Touring was there almost from the beginning and customizing grew slowly from the late Forties onwards, but the Sportster didn't arrive until 1957. Even today, Sportster riders have to suffer the odd jibe about baby bikes that aren't 'real' Harleys. And yet it's carved out a new niche in the Harley owner market consisting of riders who value at least the image of straightline performance and nimble handling.

It could have all happened twenty years earlier if the Board had been more enthusiastic about first Joe Petrali's, then Bill Harley's idea for an overhead valve 45. But first war came, then the big twins needed updating, and so implementation was delayed. When Harley-Davidson finally got round to making the Sportster, it was under duress – they had to do it to meet the threat posed by Triumph and its other competitors. But at least when the Sportster did come, it made as big a splash as the Knucklehead had twenty years before.

In fact, there's an interesting parallel with that first big ohv twin. The sporty 61E of 1936 had supplanted bigger twins that were slow and fat by comparison. But in the intervening years it too had acquired a middle-aged spread; now it was the Sportster's turn to do the same job in 1957. The 61E was launched at a time when Harleys were being relegated to the role of solid, sensible tourers. It did much to change that, but

by the late Fifties the same thing was happening all over again – it was hard to believe that the lumbering FLs were direct descendants of that original fast and flashy Knucklehead. Standards had changed too. In the 1930s it was side-valve Indians that made Harleys look cumbersome; now it was British 30ci (500cc) and 40ci (650cc) twins. They were fast, tuneable and could be flicked through S-bends like no big V-twin could. Thanks to a devaluation of the pound, they were also a lot cheaper as well.

Of course, it could be argued that bikes like these couldn't be taking sales from Harley-Davidson as they sold to a different type of rider, but Harley was still worried enough to petition the Government for tariff protection. They didn't get it, so they tried another tack. There was no question of meeting the imports head-on – Indian had already tried this with a range of underdeveloped singles and twins that were so troublesome they assisted the Wigwam to its grave.

Harley's far less radical answer was the K, a development of the old 45 side-valve V-twin in a thoroughly up to date chassis, with the foot gearchange and swinging arm rear suspension that less traditionalist riders expected. It was an odd bike – why spend all that time and money developing new running gear, only to lumber it with an out of date engine? William H. Davidson later said that the K was a stop-gap, a way of treading water until the genuinely new Sportster arrived. That sounds quite reasonable, until you realize that the Sportster took another five years to appear and that in the meantime Harley-Davidson spent more development time and money giving the K a bigger 55ci (900cc) engine when they could have been getting the

Sportster ready instead.

But in that first year or two, it wasn't really the roadburner that legend tells us it was. It had a soft 7.5:1 compression ratio and no more power than the smaller (40ci/650cc) Triumph T110. Still, the XL engine had a lot more in hand – the XLH went on sale in 1958, with a 9:1 compression, larger valves, smoother ports and aluminium tappets. The following year, all Sportsters got another power boost – higher-lift cams took it up to 55bhp at 6,800rpm. This was more like it.

At last, a Harley-Davidson that could live with the upstart Triumphs in a straight line had arrived. It was a different matter on the twisty bits, where the British bike's lower weight and legendary handling put it ahead. But the Sportster was a genuine 100mph (160km/h) road bike that wouldn't be embarrassed by impromptu Saturday night burn-outs. For some older riders, it must have seemed quite familiar – the 'Trumpet' had replaced the 'Wigwam' as arch-rival to the 'Hog'. And as before, you were on one side or the other. Sometimes these unofficial quarter-miles proved too much for the hard-worked machinery, resulting in either melted Trumpet or smoked Ham.

Saturday night heroes they might have been, but those very early Sportsters didn't really look the part. The enduring image of the Sporty is of something light and slim-looking, with a small tank and nothing that doesn't contribute to performance. But right through the Sixties it came with a big four-gallon tank and sensible valanced mudguards. Harley-Davidson seemed in two minds about the Sportster – its name and frequent power hikes sent one message, its dumpy looks another: you could even specify a screen and

panniers to turn the bike into a mini-FLH.

The bike that changed all that and gave us the classic Sportster look, was the XLCH. According to Allan Girdler, it all started with a group of Californian dealers who badgered Harley-Davidson for a stripped-down Sportster they could use in competition. Milwaukee obliged, and a couple of hundred of these XLCs (no lights or battery, and magneto ignition) were sold in 1958. From then it was an obvious move to combine the stripped-down look with the latest 9:1 engine in a road bike, the XLCH.

The result was a styling masterpiece, just as the Knucklehead had been. Everything was smaller and skimpier in order to make the engine look bigger (an old customizer's trick). The little 2.2 (10 litre) gallon tank from the 7ci (125cc) Hummer just happened to fit and it created that slimline look. The mudguards were narrower and the handlebars lower. Even the headlight was changed from an FLH-like nacelle to a smaller one tucked back between the forks, and the silencers, at first high-level, later became shorty duals. In short, all the elements that we now associate with the slim, stripped Sportster look came together with the XLCH.

As a sop to the competition aspirations, the XLCH also left the factory with semi-knobbly tyres and magneto ignition. The adverts showed the bike dashing heroically over rough ground, but it was all imagery. Most owners replaced the knobblies with proper road tyres, as well as cursing that magneto, which made starting even more of a chore than normal. And despite looking light and lithe, the XLCH still weighed in at around 500lb (136kg), so tarmac was probably the best place for it anyway. Neither did it have any more power than the standard XLH. But that

Above: *If Ida's bike is 'Hers',
this is 'His'. Husband Rick
Newman is a Sportster fan too,
and this 1964 XLH is almost
identical to Ida's, except that it's
in Fiesta Red and has the
optional spotlight kit in place of
the saddlebags and rack.*

wasn't the point; it looked like a Sportster, and
that was what it was.

If nothing else, this styling job proved that
motorcycles could sell on looks. XLCH outsold
the standard XLH by more than two to one
throughout the Sixties, and if sheer numbers are
the criterion, reached a peak of nearly 11,000 in
1973. So the Sportster in general, and the XLCH
in particular, was a good seller, but it never
managed to account for the lion's share of Harley-
Davidson sales. It was eight years before even one
in five new Harleys was a Sportster.

It did better in the Seventies, often
representing almost one-third of Harley-Davidson
total sales and this was really the low point for the
big twins, the time when big Japanese bikes were
starting to make inroads into the market, while big
Harleys hadn't yet reached the respectability
represented by the company's later model: the
Evolution (see Chapter Eight). Somehow catching
the mood of the times, the Sportster seemed the

least outdated in the Milwaukee range and for a
few years in the early 1970s, Harley actually sold
more little twins than big ones. In the peak year of
1974, helped by the American Machine &
Foundry Company-inspired production boom,
23,830 Sportsters rolled off the production line.

But a decade or so earlier, things were very
different. Harley was selling about 1,500-2,000
Sportsters a year and, though the baby twin was
doing a lot for the company image, it wasn't really
the bike that turned Harley-Davidson around.
When the Sportster came in, Harley was already
running short of capital – its sales were almost
stagnant in a booming market, and good though
the new bike was, it followed the usual pattern of
smaller bikes making smaller profits. You might
have thought that the Sportster would have opened
up sales beyond the diehard big-twin crowd and
allowed Harley-Davidson to get back into
exporting. But by the mid-1960s, when it had been
around for several years, a mere 3 per cent of
Harleys were being sent abroad. As for its effect
on the balance sheet, the best illustration is what
Harley did in 1965. It was so short of money that
for the first time this hitherto family-owned firm
went public, offering shares in the company on the
market. Even this wasn't enough, and in January
1969 Harley-Davidson was taken over by the
American Machine & Foundry Company – AMF.

But while the company wrangled on with its
internal difficulties, the Sportster was facing
challenges of its own. Although a baby by Harley
Davidson standards, the 54ci (883cc) bike was still
substantially bigger and heavier than the British
40ci (650cc) bikes. At the same time it wasn't as
nimble either, but it could usually rely on sheer
cubic capacity to win any straight-line race. This
all changed in 1968, when BSA/Triumph launched

its 45ci (750cc) triples, closely followed by big
bikes from Japan – the Honda 4 and Kawasaki's
two-stroke triples.

In fact, to compare the XLH and the Triumph
Trident, it's remarkable how closely matched they
were in almost every respect. The XLH cost
$1,753, the Trident just $3 less than that (on the
East coast). The Harley had 58bhp at 6,800rpm
from its 883cc V-twin; the higher revving 750cc
triple could manage 60bhp at 8,000. The Harley
weighed 510lb (231kg) with half a tank of fuel on
board, and the Triumph a smidgin under 500.
Cycle World tested them both in 1968 and, not
surprisingly, both turned in very similar figures.
The top-endy Triumph just pipped the Harley on
top speed (117mph/188km/h versus
114mph/183km/h), but the XLH's torque showed
up in better acceleration figures, especially at low
speeds. It needed a mere 1.8 seconds to reach
40mph/64km/h from rest (Trident, 3.1) and 4.7
seconds to 60mph/100km/h (5.6). Only when
approaching three-figure speeds did the Triumph
finally manage to get past, although it has to be
said that in particular XLH was almost
suspiciously fast. If true, the figures would have
made it quicker than the 70bhp XR1000. Certainly
the previous 55bhp XLH tested by *Cycle World*
would have lagged behind any Trident, so we can
probably safely stick with the view that the later
Sportster and Triumph triple were very closely
matched.

In any event, Harley-Davidson evidently
thought the figures were too close for comfort, and
in 1972 bored the Sportster out to just under
1,000cc – the 61ci Harley had returned. The
company claimed only a small power increase to
61bhp at 6,200rpm, but didn't quote any torque
figures. That was rather odd, as surely the

Sportster's better torque had to be its main advantage over the revvier opposition. Still, *Cycle World* found it could top 116mph (187km/h) and run a 13.38 second standing quarter, which was probably enough for most people.

That latest XLCH was still demonstrably a Harley, but the next variation on the Sportster theme was very different indeed. It was deliberately styled *not* to look like a Harley-

Davidson at all. It was another product of Willie G. Davidson's styling department, which had already come up with the successful 1970 Super Glide. Grandson of the original Davidson generation, Willie G. had joined the styling department after a short stint outside the family firm. It's hard to believe now, but this bearded, denim-clad ambassador for bikers once wore a collar, tie and sensible haircut to work every day.

Its designer's haircut notwithstanding, the Super Glide was a reasonably streetwise bike, a mildly-chopped big twin that brought official recognition to what customizers had been doing to their Harleys for years. It opened up a whole new market for Harley-Davidson – factory customization.

Now he wanted to do the same again with a café racer Harley: the Sportster-based XLCR was

the result. This was a *real* departure – the bikini fairing, flat bars and single seat all pointed in the right direction, though it was hardly radical by café racer standards. But by Harley standards it was – in silhouette it might even, horror of horrors, be taken for something else. There was hardly a glint of chrome on the XLCR, which took its black on black colour scheme right down to the matt black exhaust system. There had never been a Harley-Davidson with less chrome.

Mechanically, the café Harley did the same clever thing as the Super Glide, mixing and matching standard Harley-Davidson components with a few deft bits of glassfibre styling to create a completely new look. The front half of the frame was Sportster and the rear end derived

from the XR750 racer. The fibreglass pointy tailpiece showed XR750 influence too, and was balanced at the front by a skimpy front mudguard and that obligatory headlamp fairing. Engine-wise, it was the standard 998cc Sportster engine, with a couple of tweaks to the ignition and exhaust system to give 68bhp at 6,200rpm. Lower gearing than was standard on the Sportster meant a slightly lower top speed and slightly quicker acceleration, but the engine was by now effectively obsolete – like every other Harley, the Sportster was selling not for what it did, but for what it stood for. It was overdue for a change.

Left: *Mechanically, the XLCR's engine was a standard 61ci (1000cc) Sportster, but with the addition of the obligatory black bits to blend in with the new machine's café racer image.*

Opposite: *Jerri Grindle is the third owner of this particular XLCR which was number 506 out of 3,301 produced. It is standard apart from the addition of an oil cooler.*

Specifications

1957 XL/1972 XLCH 1000

Engine	OHV, 45-degree V-twin
Bore x stroke	XL: 3in x 3.81in (76.2 x 96.8mm) XLCH: 3.19 x 3.81in (81.0 x 96.8mm)
Capacity	XL: 53.9ci (883cc) XLCH: 60.9ci (998cc)
Compression ratio	XL: 7.5:1 XLCH 9.0:1
Carburettor	XL: Linkert XLCH: Bendix-Zenith $1^{21}/_{32}$ in
Lubrication	Dry sump with gear-type pump
Ignition	Battery and coil
Power	XL 40 bhp @ 5,500 rpm XLCH 55 bhp @ 6,800 rpm

Gearbox	Four-speed, constant mesh, unit construction
Gear ratios	(XLCH) 1st: 11.16:1 2nd: 8.08:1 3rd 6.11:1 4th 4.42:1
Clutch	XL: dry multi-plate XLCH: wet multi-plate
Primary drive	Triplex chain,
Final drive	Chain
Suspension	
Front	Telescopic forks
Rear	Swinging arm with twin hydraulic dampers
Wheels/tyres	4.00 x 19in
Front	XL: 3.50 x 18in XLCH: 3.75 x 19in
Rear	4.25 x 18in
Brakes	
Front	Drum, 8.0 x 1.5in
Rear	Drum, 8.0 x 1.0in
Wheelbase	58.5in (149cm)

Seat height	29.7in (75cm)
Fuel capacity	XL: 4.4 gallons (20 litres) XLCH: 2.2 gallons (10 litres)
Fuel consumption	43 mpg (15 ltr/km)
Oil capacity	6 pints (3.4 litres)
Performance	XLCH was tested by Cycle World February 1972
Top Speed	116.2 mph (187 km/h)
Speeds in gears (theoretical @ 6,500 rpm)	
	1st 45mph (72km/h)
	2nd 62mph (100km/h)
	3rd 82mph (132km/h)
	4th 113mph (182km/h)
0-60 mph	5.5 secs
Standing quarter	13.38 secs
Kerb weight	XLCH: 492lb (223kg)

Chapter Eight
Evolution: Revolution?

It's tempting to think that Evolution, the cleaned up, modernized V-twin engine that has carried Harley's fortunes since 1983, was a post-AMF engine. Freed from the shackles of stifling bureaucracy, the courageous buy-back team went back to basics; they rode home to Milwaukee from York, Pennsylvania and came up with an as American as apple pie V-twin. A nice story, but not true. The Evolution, Evo, V2 or Blockhead, whatever you want to call it, was actually a product of the AMF era.

Much has been written about Harley's AMF period which stretched from 1969 up to the celebrated buy-back of 1981. For some, the American Machine & Foundry Company was a grey-faced asset stripper which knew little about motorcycles and cared less. It greedily doubled production in order to squeeze profit out of Harley-Davidson, only to find that quality nosedived as a result. When the fast buck didn't work, it hastily pulled out.

There is some truth in that version of events, but not much. AMF certainly didn't know much about bikes or it would have realized that Harley-Davidsons of the Seventies were outdated, unreliable things that you had to be a diehard to buy. And it did double the production rate without much regard for quality. But it certainly wasn't after a quick return – AMF stuck with Harley-Davidson for twelve years and put a lot of money into re-equipping its own York plant in Pennsylvania for bike assembly, while Milwaukee built engines and gearboxes. It should also be worth noting that Bangor Punta, AMF's only rival in the bidding for America's last motorcycle manufacturer, really did have a track record of asset stripping. The consensus seems to be that if Harley-Davidson had been taken over by Bangor

Right: *In America, the Evolution-engined Harley has become* the *custom bike. The Evo is reliable and leak-free, but it also looks good and makes the right noises – just right for a slow-cruising custom bike.*

Opposite: *Few custom bikes can claim to have been inspired by a pair of $3 sunglasses, but Steven Minunni's was. Called, appropriately enough 'Cheap Sunglasses', this black and silver bike was painted by its owner.*

Punta, it probably wouldn't be around today.

If nothing else, AMF left Harley-Davidson alive and intact and with far more modern capacity than it had before. What AMF failed to realize (until it was too late) was that the key priority for Harley-Davidson was not mass production, but new product. Only with an up-to-date bike of the right quality could it afford to increase production. Even now, a decade down the line with Harley-Davidson looking more secure than it has done for years, production has settled to around 45,000-50,000 bikes a year, a far cry from the mid-1970s peak of 75,000. The company has reached that happy point of keeping production just below demand – not a bad recipe for corporate health.

It wasn't until 1978 that AMF seemed to realize where it was going wrong. Ten million dollars had been spent on an 1100cc version of the venerable Shovelhead V-twin, which as well as being basically troublesome and prone to oil leaks, looked unlikely to pass the looming new laws on emissions and noise levels. The Shovelhead was a dirty, noisy engine from another era – it had to go.

The man to grasp the nettle was Vaughn Beals, who was put into Milwaukee by AMF in early 1976. His first act was to send a group of senior managers on a week-long brain-storming session to come up with a long-term plan for the company. They were unanimous: Harley had to have a much improved version of the V-twin to keep its traditional market.

In the longer term, a whole family of engines was needed. Beals approved, AMF approved, and work began. The new V-twin would be developed in-house, but the new family (code-named NOVA) was farmed out to Porsche.

Harley-Davidson didn't have the resources (nor it must be said, the experience of truly modern engines) to do this job. NOVA certainly looked ambitious, being a range of engines from a 30ci (500cc) twin to an 80ci (1300cc) six, all of them water-cooled.

It all looked very promising as Harley-Davidson was at last being allowed to work towards a long-term goal, rather than being compelled to chase weekly production targets. There were incremental changes to the bikes, too – 1980 was a big year of change, with a rubber mounting being introduced to calm the vibratory effects of the engine as well as a belt drive and a five-speed gearbox.

Unfortunately, AMF's new Chief Executive Officer Tom York was looking askance at NOVA, which had already swallowed $10 million. He could also see that Harley-Davidson's share of the big bike market had slumped from 77 per cent in 1973 to little more than 30 per cent by 1980, and that the company made up 17 per cent of AMF's turnover, but only 1 per cent of its profits. So when Vaughn Beals suggested a management buy-out, he agreed, though it took months long of negotiation before the deal was eventually finalized.

For the new engine programme, this meant the cancellation of the NOVA project; the new team started out owing many millions to assorted banks, leaving the revamped twin as the company's only new engine. If Harley-Davidson was worried by its by now forced reliance on the Evolution, it needn't have been. Not only was the new engine reliable and oil-tight, it was trouble-free from the start. For Harley-Davidson, that was a novel experience: it was many years since Harley had got a new engine right first time.

The Harley-Davidson engineers appeared to have started, not with grand ideas, but by pinpointing exactly what was wrong with the old engine. In the summer of 1978 they made a detailed study of warranty claims and service problems on the Shovelhead, and the result was an all-new top end. The old bottom end was retained almost unchanged though, which speeded things up a great deal and meant that they were able to build up the prototypes very quickly – the first ones were running by late 1978. Then followed the second reason for the Evo's pain-free introduction. It spent 5,600 hours on the test bench and 750,000 miles (1207,000km) on the road before it was passed fit for production. It's unlikely that any other Harley engine received such a painstaking development, with the possible exception of the Founders' first single.

So what was actually new about it? The con-rods were thicker at their base, and Harley-Davidson claimed for them a fatigue life ten times longer than those of the Shovelhead. Bore and stroke were the same as the old engine, but the cylinder barrels changed from cast iron to aluminium alloy, with iron liners – that meant less weight and cooler running (Harley claimed 75 per cent improved heat dissipation). Heads and barrels were clamped to the crankcase by long through-bolts, a more rigid arrangement than the previous system of short, separate studs that had been used for both components.

German flat-top pistons from Mahle were used. They had an 8.5:1 compression ratio (well up on the Shovelhead's), but the new engine could operate without detonation. Marginally lighter than the Shovelhead's, the new pistons had different contours top and bottom to allow for the crown's greater expansion. The idea was that the piston would expand and become round as the engine heated up, and at the same rate as the bore. That, it was intended, would allow closer tolerances, quieter running and lower oil consumption. In fact, reducing oil use was one of the project's main aims – older Shovels had the habit of pooling oil around the valve guides from where it would be sucked into the combustion chamber when the valve opened and burnt. The Evo allowed excess oil to drain back down the head/barrel bolts, pushrod tubes and tappet blocks, to be recycled.

But the biggest changes came in the cylinder heads themselves. The valve angle was narrower (58 degrees) and the ports smaller and straighter – an improvement on those in the Shovelhead which limited power. The valves were smaller to suit and had milder timing, though their lift was greater. Smaller valves brought the usual benefit of higher gas velocity, especially at low engine speeds, which helped torque. As a side benefit they were also lighter than before, which together with the lighter (hollow) pushrods made the valve-train safe to a higher rpm – the Evo could rev to 6,400rpm. The tappets were still hydraulic, but they had wider rollers and the cams were computer designed: a first for Harley-Davidson. Ignition was electronic, of course, but with the extra sophistication of a two-stage advance curve. On small throttle openings, the engine ran with 50 degrees BTDC (good for economy) but at higher loads it reduced to 32 degrees, (preventing detonation).

But did it all work? The short answer was *yes*. The Evo was lighter than the old engine, said by Harley-Davidson to produce 10 per cent more power and 15 per cent more torque. It was quieter,

easier to service and didn't leak or drink oil. But best of all, it still looked and sounded like a Harley-Davidson engine. With the Evolution, Harley seemed to have struck the right balance between character and modern convenience, and was sensibly ducking out of the horsepower race. As Vaughn Beals said at the original press launch, 'We know that quarter-mile and high speed isn't our game, and we don't want the four valves [per cylinder] and four carbs and $200 tune-up that comes with that type of performance. We want something a shade-tree mechanic can take care of.' What a shade-tree mechanic would have made of the two-stage electronic ignition, Beals didn't say, but you could appreciate the sentiment.

For the time being, the new engine came as a 1340cc big twin only; from November 1983 it was

fitted to the three F-series touring bikes (the Tour Glide, the Electra Glide and the Sport Glide), the FXRS Low Glide and the first Softail. *Cycle World* tested the new engine in a Tour Glide, finding it a second quicker over the quarter mile and eager to pull round to the red line at 5,500rpm – this was new for an 80ci Harley-Davidson twin.

Apologies must go to any reader not turned on by the nut and bolt intricacies of an engine. But it's worth spending time examining the Evo because it has been so pivotal in Harley's recent history. It's no exaggeration to say that this engine saved the company – the Shovelhead was nearing the end of its life, not just from the point of view of noise and emissions, but because it seemed so crude compared with its competitors. The all-new NOVA range was still years away from launch,

even assuming the newly independent Harley-Davidson could have funded its development.

Not only did the Evo come along at the right time, it was also perfectly placed to take advantage of the way the motorcycle market was developing. Buyers were increasingly older and more affluent than they had been. Many were more interested in style than performance and as the 1980s progressed there was a movement back towards such 'character' motorcycles. Whether it was a dash of nostalgia, or a backlash against the perceived blandness of modern bikes, Harley-Davidson benefited, and has done ever since.

Not that it was all plain sailing for the newly independent Harley-Davidson, however. The eagle might be soaring once again, but there was no guarantee it wouldn't crash-land. When

Right: *With the emphasis on finish there seem to be few apparent changes apart from a 5-degree rake for the extended forks. Unlike many custom bikes, Terminator's owner does not use many after-market parts – it's all Harley.*

Below: *Paint and chrome have won prizes in Quebec, Chicago and Columbus, while at the 1996 Rat's Hole Show at Daytona the bike was placed sixth out of seventy-five in the stock class.*

Opposite: *Pool-side custom in the lowrider/café style. The most obvious engine change to this one is the twin choke carburettor: it's possible but expensive to fit twin carbs to an Evolution, so twin chokes are more commonplace.*

negotiations over the buy-back began in 1980, the company had just over 30 per cent of the big 851cc plus bike market. The year after that it lost leadership, for the first time in decades, to Honda; and in 1983, when the Evo was announced, the company's market share slumped to a low of 23.3 per cent. Only in 1984, three years after the buy-back, did the recovery begin; Harley managed to gain 26.9 per cent of the big bikes market that

year. As the market improved, and word got round that with the Evo, Harley really had got it right this time, the company's recovery gathered pace – by 1988 the V-twins were grabbing a 46.8 per cent share and Harley-Davidson made a profit of $27 million.

Not all of this was down to the Evolution, crucial though the new model was. Harley-Davidson had always been a conservative

company, but it now seemed willing, even eager, to find new ways of making bikes and chasing sales. Whether it was the near-collapse in 1981, or the stark reality of being responsible for its own destiny, Harley-Davidson was now open to innovation as never before. Three new ideas (new to traditional American industry at any rate) – just-in-time inventory management, employee involvement and statistical operator control –

Right: *While a few bodywork bikes have totally enclosed the engines, fewer still have worked aesthetically: the whole point of a custom Harley is that the engine is the centrepiece.*

Below right: *Bodywork bikes are definitely a 1990s branch of the custom movement. They are the antithesis of the lean and rangy chopper: everything smooth, faired and elegant. This one seems inspired by 1950s sci-fi – if Dan Dare had ridden a Harley, this would surely have been it!*

worked wonders with both productivity and quality improvement. There was a new policy of getting as many potential buyers as possible actually onto bikes – a test fleet did the rounds of the bike shows.

But all of the JIT initiatives and the test rides wouldn't have mattered a hoot without the right product. It's ironic that the Evolution, originally seen as a stop-gap design, is still the basis of Harley's current success. When it was launched, Harley also gave a preview of a new V4, said to be the next new engine. Well, here we are sixteen years later and there's still no sign of it. But with the 'stop-gap' Evo having carved out such an effective and profitable niche, they really don't need a new engine. Or do they?

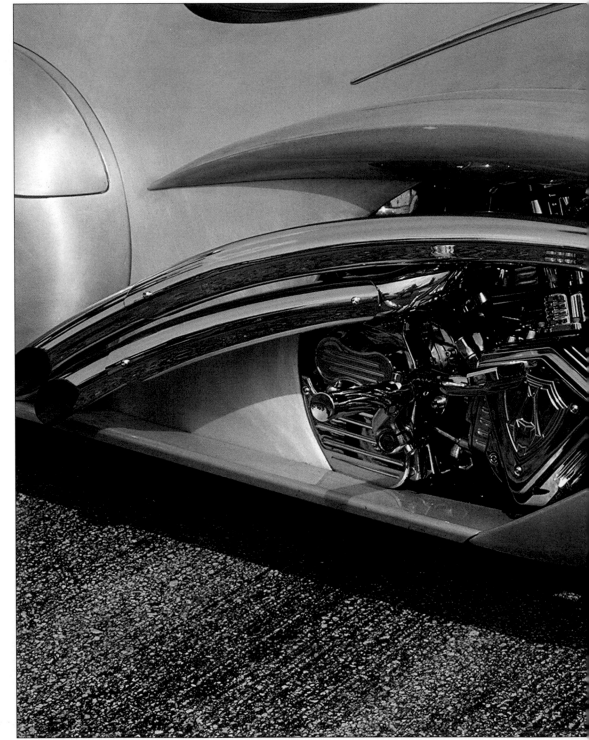

Opposite top: *That rear light is actually from a 1949 Ford, and it helped Donnie Smith and his friends to achieve the sort of look they were aiming for: a low-riding, classy-looking bodywork bike.*

Opposite below: *Sheryl Emede poses with Donnie Smith, a well-known name in customizing, whose bikes have a retro feel which blends well with Harley's own backwards-looking styling.*

Specifications

1983 FLHTC Electra Glide

Engine	OHV, 45-degree V-twin
Bore x stroke	88.8 x 108mm
Capacity	82ci (1340cc)
Compression ratio	8.5:1
Carburettor	Keihin 38mm
Ignition	Electronic inductive, two-stage advance
Lubrication	Dry sump
Power	71.5 bhp @ 5,000 rpm
Torque	82.5lb ft @ 3,600 rpm
Gearbox	Five-speed, constant-mesh
Gear ratios	1st: 10.45:1 2nd: 7.13:1 3rd: 5.17:1 4th: 3.98:1 5th: 3.22:1
Clutch	Wet multi-plate
Primary drive	Duplex chain,
Final drive	Enclosed chain in oil bath
Suspension	
Front	Telescopic fork (4.6in travel)
Rear	Swinging arm, twin hydraulic dampers (3.6in travel)
Wheels/tyres	
Front	MT90-16
Rear	MT90-16
Brakes	
Front	Twin discs, 11.5in
Rear	Discs, 12in
Wheelbase	63in (160cm)

Seat height	30$\frac{1}{2}$in (77cm)
Fuel capacity	5 gallons (23 litres)
Fuel consumption	47 mpg (17 ltr/km)
Performance	FLHTC was tested by Cycle World November 1983
Top Speed	96 mph (154km/h)
Speeds in gears (theoretical @ 6,500 rpm)	
	1st 38mph (61km/h)
	2nd 56mph (90km/h)
	3rd 78mph (126km/h)
	4th 101mph (163km/h)
0-60 mph	6.9 secs
Kerb weight	762lb (346kg)

Chapter Nine
Softails & Springers: Profiting from the Past

Nostalgia has become big business. It could be down to the collapse of the post-war political order, or economic uncertainties, or simply that the West has an ageing population. Whatever the reason, more people seem to enjoy harking back to a supposedly golden age than ever before. At least, that's the impression.

Take music: we've had the Fifties Rock 'n' Roll revival; fond memories of Sixties love and peace; while from the 1970s, punk (seen as the end of civilized society at the time) is having its own second time around. And no doubt the children of the Eighties will in their turn bemoan all this 'modern music'. But, rather like nostalgia itself, all of this is somewhat selective – the point is that we have an opportunity to enjoy a taste of the times, the best bits rather than the reality of the whole. And that's exactly what Harley-Davidson has been doing with its motorcycles for the last ten years.

It was probably sometime in the Seventies that Harley-Davidson gave up trying to make its bikes look modern. The Sportster was given its derided 'boat-tail' rear end in 1970. Then there was the XLCR Café Racer, that attempt to make a Milwaukee twin look like other bikes. But these attempts failed – the boat-tails were as often as not thrown into the back of the garage, and in its sole year, the XLCR was outsold by the traditional Sportster by more than ten to one.

If there was a lesson to learn, Harley-Davidson took it on board. The FXS Low Rider of 1977 pointed the true way forward. With its low-stepped seat, sissy bar and high pegs, it looked every inch the authentic, low-riding custom bike, except that it came direct from the factory, ready-made and ready to go. Harley sold

nearly 10,000 of them in 1979 and got the message – styling sells.

Until the Evolution engine came along, restyling was what they had to do to keep the old machinery selling. The Sportster got a back-to-basics revival with 1983's all-black XLX version. Now this couldn't have been more different from the Café Racer: it was deliberately styled to look exactly how everyone thought a Sportster *should* look. The single seat, the tiny (just over two gallons/9 litres) fuel tank and the stripped down naked look all referred back, not to the very first Sportster, but to the XLCH, the first Sportster with the looks to match its name.

It was, according to *Cycle World*, 'an elemental motorcycle, stark in its simplicity.' It also re-established the Sportster's image as a stripped-down Harley, the lightweight counterpart of the big tourers. Of course, in real performance terms it had long since been left behind by the Japanese sports bikes, but that didn't matter: the look did.

There was another, more practical, aspect to the XLX. Its $3,995 price tag was an attempt by Milwaukee to make an entry-level bike, something which could compete with the Big Four on price as well as image. There seemed to be a realization that to keep making bikes in sensible numbers, Harley-Davidson had to avoid retreating into an upmarket ghetto. So it had to offer something that non-Harley riders could afford, and which they would consider buying.

This was even more true of the Sportster 883. In 1985, Harley-Davidson took the logical step of making a smaller version of the Evo engine – the same all-alloy top end on the Sportster's existing unit construction bottom half. Technically, it offered all the advances of the Evo

1340; it was oil-tight, quiet and reliable. And despite its smaller size, it produced just as much power as the XLX's 61ci (1,000cc) Shovelhead. Harley-Davidson might say that the sub-900 size put it into a lower insurance bracket, which it did; but it also evoked memories of the original Sportster, which had been an 883 for years.

This latest basic Sportster seemed to revel in its simplicity. All the improvements the bigger Harleys were enjoying, such as the five-speed gearboxes, belt drives and rubber-mounted engines, were omitted. There was a lone speedometer (no rev counter) and the bike came in simple, solid colours – red, black or yellow. Even the 'Harley-Davidson' lettering on the tank was in a simple white script: no grandiose badges here. The result was a return to the original price tag of the XLX, which had since crept beyond its

Left: *The modern Sportster. The 883 Evolution Sportster has done more to bring a new generation of riders into Harley ownership than any other. Road testers weren't always impressed, but it was close to the Japanese custom bikes on price and it had a lot more image to offer.*

Left: *Dan Grannan owns this 1990 Softail Custom which won Best of Show at Laconia Bike Week in 1995. Turbo Graphics did the paintwork. The rear mudguard looks like a Ness Taildragger but was actually handmade.*

Right: *Outside the Ocean Centre in Daytona, Gilles Marcoux's bike shows a different sort of style. Unlike the Fat Boy-derived solidity of the previous bike, this one is skinny and spare, more like the traditional high-barred chopper.*

Opposite left: *This bike's engine was built up by Leo Harley-Davidson, the Montreal dealer. Long gone are the days when Harley dealers refused to have anything to do with custom bikes.*

Opposite right: *Although there's a dazzling array of off-the-shelf custom bits, many customizers now prefer to hand-make parts. On this bike, the mudguards, dash, exhaust, front brake cover and number plate were all handmade.*

entry-level aspirations. The new 883, Evolution engine and all, was $700 cheaper. When it was launched, Vaughn Beals promised that Harley-Davidson would hang on to that low price as long as possible.

And it did. It was the same price two years later when Harley took the remarkable step of guaranteeing that you would receive that same retail price when you came to trade the bike in. It was an amazing statement of faith in the 883's residual value – trade the bike in within two years, and you were guaranteed exactly the same as you paid for it. It was only possible because Harley-Davidson's revival was well under way by then and secondhand values were on the up anyway. There was a catch: the offer only applied if you traded your 883 in for an FL or FX Harley, the ones with bigger price tags and fatter profit margins. It worked, and the 883 succeeded in drawing a new generation into Harley-Davidson ownership.

However, though the 883 looked like a neat and updated variation on a classic theme, apparent claims didn't always stand up to close scrutiny. By the late Eighties, every Japanese factory was fielding its own 750cc-800cc V-twin custom/cruiser, all for about the same price as the 883. *Cycle World* tested them all in 1988 and was unimpressed enough to place the Harley last. It was too slow, too uncomfortable and too vibratory, though of course it was worth a lot when you came to sell it. As a marketing success, or even as a means of making Harley-Davidson ownership more affordable, you couldn't find fault with the 883, but it wasn't a modern bike.

For riding, the new Sportster 1200 made a lot more sense. Bored out to 89mm (the same as the big twins) it produced 68bhp at 6,000rpm and

72lb ft at 4,000rpm. In a world where superbikes had 130bhp or more, the Sportster must have seemed like a throwback. Fortunately, its mid-range torque gave a very quick and, responsive top-gear acceleration (40mph-60mph/65km/h-96km/h in 3.6 seconds) which peakier revving rivals could seldom match. Here was a Sportster that, in one sense at least, deserved its name. Little wonder that one of the most popular modifications to the 883 Harley was upping the capacity to 1200cc.

Even so, performance wasn't necessarily the first thing on most riders' minds when they bought a new Sportster. They bought it because it was more specifically a Harley, and because it had been deliberately styled to look like a particular type of Harley. The 1980s saw Harley-Davidson work the same trick with its bigger bikes. The FL family, the range of traditional tourers that still used the Electra Glide name, carried serenely on, selling to the same clientele it always had; but there was a fresh market for

big Harleys which the company was about to top with a new model.

It had its genesis in the Super Glide of 1970 and the later Low Rider: it was quite distinct from the Sportster and tourer lines. The design may have started off as the first factory custom, but it reached its logical conclusion in the unashamed nostalgia of the Softail. With its rear suspension well-hidden to give a hard tail-look, the Softail was different from the Sportster and the FL. Their old profiles had been carefully, perhaps artificially, maintained: the Softail was a 1950s-look bike designed in the Eighties.

The inspiration came not from Harley-Davidson's Design Department, but from an independent engineer named Bill Davis. He had built a bike which featured dual shock absorbers hidden horizontally under the gearbox and linked to a triangulated swinging arm. It worked well enough for him to patent it and when Vaughn Beals saw the system at a rally, he liked it enough to buy the rights.

The result was the FXST Softail of 1983. Like Bill Davis's original bike, the two gas dampers were mounted under the gearbox; unlike conventional suspension systems, they were extended (not compressed) as the rear wheel moved upwards over bumps. They gave four inches of travel (about the same as conventionally suspended Harleys); the only complaint was that they were set up for soft, boulevard cruising and so bottomed out quickly on poor surfaces. All the extra metalwork meant the Softail also weighed 30lb (14kg) more than the standard bike and cost a lot more as well. But the buyers loved it: so much so that it was Harley's best-selling bike in 1984 and the company had to up the production run several times to keep pace with demand.

The secret of this success wasn't just in the rear end's authentic spine-jarring look. Other features (or lack of them) sought to make the Softail out as a 'real' motorcycle. It eschewed the rubber engine mounting, the five-speed gearbox and the belt drive of 'modern' Harleys. This wasn't to save money, as the Sportster had done, but to provide some authentic engine vibes to match the bike's retrospective rear end: it even had a kickstart to back up the perfectly adequate electrics. The traditional Fat Bob tank was back too – two 2.6 gallon tanks, one on either side of the frame, and each with its own chrome-plated filler. The wheels were spoked of course (not alloy) while buckhorn handlebars, highway pegs and a skinny 21-inch front tyre completed the bike's chopper profile. There were innumerable stylistic details like the small headlamp, bobbed rear mudguard and the careful use of chrome: they all added up to an overall look that made the Softail a huge success.

In fact, the only part of the Softail which was obviously modern were the Japanese telescopic forks. Harley-Davidson put that right in 1986 with the Heritage Softail. Essentially, it did the same for the front suspension as the Softail frame had done for the rear – it made the modern elements look old by disguising them. This time, the forks were hidden behind massive shrouds which made the bike a spitting image of the original, pre-new fangled rear suspension, Panhead. Again, it was a sham, and again the buyers loved it.

Two years later, Harley-Davidson came up with yet another variation on the Softail theme. The Springer Softail was different. Where the other Softies succeeded in looking old by hiding their modern bits, the Springer achieved the same end by recreating them. Quite simply, Harley-Davidson produced a new set of leading-link springer forks, just like the ones Bill Harley had designed in 1907. At the launch, there was a lot of talk about modern materials and computer-aided design, but Harley-Davidson wasn't fooling anyone: the new Springers had less than four inches of travel where most Harleys with conventional front forks had six or seven. The front tyre was a 21-inch item a mere 2.15 inches across. None of this boded well for a bike that

Right: *Buells have come a long way from their racer origins. The original XR1000-based RR1000 was a slow seller because it was a little too racer-like for its market, but the later RS and RSS versions were more like Harley-Davidson sports tourers.*

Opposite left: *The design of this, the latest Buell, is clearly inspired by European bikes like the Ducati Monstro and Triumph Speed Triple. Like all Buells, the idea is to marry Harley's V-twin to a high performance chassis.*

Opposite right: *Donnie Smith specializes in bodywork and he produced the tank, fenders and air dam on this bike, as well as the handle bars and exhaust pipes.*

weighed over 600lb (272kg), though, when *Cycle World* tested the Springer (or FXSTS, to give it its factory designation) it was impressed. The new fork was found to soak up small ripples better than telescopics, with less dive on heavy braking, though it could bottom out on bigger bumps.

But whether the Springers 'new' forks performed better or worse than their predecessors wasn't really the point. They looked the part, even though this time there was no attempt by Harley-Davidson to style the rest of the bike to suit them. It was all virtually unchanged from the original Softail design, though the hidden rear dampers did get pre-load adjustment. Before, they were too soft and ready to bottom out with average-weight riders. Now, as road testers ruefully pointed out, adjusting the pre-load to suit made the ride rather harsh. But as with the Springers, this didn't seem to matter to those who were signing cheques in the showroom. In fact, eight years on, the Springer Softail is still part of the range, despite the fact that in Britain it costs over £12,600 – about the same as a mid-range family car.

But that only goes to prove what a rich vein of business Harley was tapping. Not for nothing was it able to charge an extra $500 for the Softail Custom – $500 for a disc rear wheel, a black-painted engine and a sissy bar. And it didn't have to stop when you took delivery: for most Harley owners, that was just the start of a long process of adding accessories and optional extras to get just the look they wanted. Harley-Davidson, with its new-found marketing acumen, was making more use than ever of the *Genuine Harley-Davidson Accessories Catalog*. The company had long made money out of accessories – Harley-Davidson sweaters, complete with logo, were offered in the 1920s – but part and parcel of the company's recent revival has been an explosion in its accessories business.

Take the Heritage Softail. If you didn't think it had quite enough period feel, you could bolt on a solo sprung saddle. Studded leather saddle-bags go with the image too, as do twin passing-lights, a chrome luggage-rack, a 2-into-1 fishtail exhaust and so on. The possibilities weren't quite endless: it just seemed as though they were. Harley-Davidson would even repaint the bike for you, though nobody lives very far from a competent paintshop. Simply send tank and mudguards back to the factory with a few hundred dollars, and they come back with a retro two-tone colour scheme. It helped, of course, that increasing numbers of Harley customers were mature 'born again' bikers with money to spend and a taste for nostalgia. More than anyone else, they shaped Harley's range in the 1980s and 1990s. For better or worse, it looks as if they'll carry on doing so for a while yet.

Specifications

1989 Springer Softail FX

Engine	OHV, 45-degree V-twin
Bore x stroke	88 x 108mm
Capacity	1339cc
Compression ratio	8.5:1
Carburettor	38mm Keihin CV
Power	70 bhp @ 5,000 rpm
Torque	80lb @ 4,000 rpm
Gearbox	Five-speed, constant-mesh
Gear ratios	1st: 10.93:1 2nd: 7.45:1 3rd: 5.40:1 4th: 4.16:1 5th: 3.37:1
Clutch	Wet multi-plate
Primary drive	Duplex chain,
Final drive	Chain
Suspension	
Front	Harley-Davidson leading-link forks
Rear	Showa twin hydraulic dampers, mounted horizontally
Wheels/tyres	
Front	MH90-21
Rear	MT90-16
Wheelbase	65in (165cm)
Seat height	26¹⁄₂in (67cm)
Fuel capacity	4.6 gallons (21 litres)
Performance	Tested by Cycle World February 1989
Top Speed	116 mph (187km/h)
Speeds in gears (theoretical @ 5,200 rpm)	
1st	36mph (60km/h)
2nd	52mph (85km/h)
3rd	77mph (124km/h)
4th	95mph (153km/h)
5th	117mph (188km/h)
0-60 mph	5.2 secs
60-80mph in 5th gear	4.7 secs
Standing quarter-mile	14.15 secs
Kerb weight	629lb (290kg)

Index